CRYPTIDS OF THE WORLD, WHERE LEGENDS MEET REALITY

EXPLORE THE LEGENDS AND MYSTERIES OF HIDDEN CREATURES THROUGH EVIDENCE AND EYEWITNESS REPORTS

KAREN E. MUELLER, DVM

CONTENTS

INTRODUCTION

The Mothman

In the quiet town of Point Pleasant, West Virginia, a strange figure was seen in the dark skies in November 1966. Two young couples driving along a lonely road claimed to have seen a creature with glowing red eyes and massive wings. They later described it as six to seven feet tall and kind of like a human in appearance, except for the wings and the eyes. It rose like a helicopter and chased after their car, making a screeching sound. The sighting was the first of a series of encounters with what came to be known as the Mothman. This fleeting encounter adds to the growing collection of stories and sightings that fuel our fascination with cryptids.

Welcome to a journey where legends meet reality. This book explores the mysterious realm of cryptids—creatures on the very edge of our understanding. Here, we blend storytelling with evidence, examining the lore and eyewitness accounts that keep the mystery alive. From the elusive Sasquatch to the enigmatic Loch Ness Monster, these creatures captivate and intrigue us, inviting believers and skeptics to explore their existence.

As for me, I am Dr. Karen Mueller, a veterinarian with 34 years of practice. I have spent my career working with small animals, the animals we know. Yet my passion for the unknown has led me to study Sasquatch encounters. Over the past five years, I have listened to countless cryptology podcasts, followed explorers' journeys on YouTube, and read numerous books on cryptids. In 2024, I condensed behaviors from thousands of eyewitness encounters into a book on Sasquatch behavior. My background and experiences provide a unique lens through which I explore these creatures, and this work has fueled my belief that there is much more yet to discover.

Cryptids are creatures whose existence is suggested but has not been scientifically proven. They occupy a fascinating space where myth, science, and mystery intersect. In folklore, they are the stuff of legends. In contemporary culture, they challenge our perceptions of what is real. They represent our curiosity and our desire to reveal mysteries.

Throughout history, people from diverse cultures have shared tales of cryptids. These stories are woven into the fabric of human storytelling and belief systems. They tap into universal themes of the unknown and the unexplained, reflecting our collective fascination with the mysteries that lie beyond our grasp.

This book will explore many cryptids, from well-known legends like Bigfoot and the Loch Ness Monster to lesser-known creatures like the Ningen, Grootslang, and Bunyip. We will also explore legends that are more ghostlike but overlap with cryptids in many of their characteristics, such as La Llorona, El Silbón, and the Hawaiian Night Marchers. Each chapter offers a glimpse into the world of these hidden and/or mystic beings, providing context and insight into their cultural significance.

This approach combines folklore discussion, scientific investigation, and contemporary evidence. It relies on credible sources and eyewitness testimonies to build a comprehensive narrative. By examining these elements, the aim is to provide a balanced exploration that respects both the mystery and the pursuit of truth.

As you read, I encourage you to keep an open mind. Consider the possibilities these creatures present. What if some of them genuinely exist? How would that change our understanding of the world? Would it make a difference to you the next time you go out in the woods, hiking, camping, or fishing? For educators, this book offers creative strategies to inspire and use critical thinking and scientific inquiry through the exploration of cryptids.

The images in this book are originals that I created using AI. They resulted from many hours of fine-tuning to obtain the pictures that I felt represented each cryptid well. Some images are based on descriptions from eyewitness sightings, such as Bigfoot (Sasquatch) and Yeti. Many others have never been seen clearly or may not even exist. In addition, some cryptids, such as the Australian Bunyip, have directly conflicting descriptions, such as an elongated neck and part ox, part hippo, or somewhat like a human; in this case, with some prompting, AI came up with a cryptid image that seemed appropriately terrifying to me.

I have searched social media for supportive videos and eyewitness testimonies. You will find notations about what I have found at the end of each cryptid segment. Of course, new posts are always available, so please look on your own if you're interested in something in particular. Also, see the references at the end of the book for suggestions on where to look further.

I invite you to delve into the chapters that follow. Together, we will explore an array of creatures that defy explanation, promising an exploration that is both enlightening and exciting. Let us question, wonder, and perhaps even believe in the mysteries that await.

ONE
THE ORIGINS OF CRYPTIDS

The Sphinx of Giza

THROUGHOUT ANCIENT HISTORY, stories of mythical beasts captured people's imaginations and became an important part of culture and belief. In ancient Mesopotamia, early concepts of dragons began to emerge. These powerful, snake-like, winged creatures originated from Babylonian myths and represented chaos and destruction, reflecting the fears of a society grappling with the unpredictable forces of nature.

In the deserts of Egypt, the Sphinx—featuring the body of a lion and the head of a human—guarded the secrets of the pyramids. This exemplified the Egyptians' fascination with hybrid creatures. In Greece, the Chimera— a fire-breathing monster with the heads of a lion, goat, and serpent— symbolized the strange and supernatural, challenging the boundaries of what was known.

The Leviathan

1.1 ANCIENT LEGENDS AND MYTHICAL BEASTS

Cryptid legends have their roots in early civilizations, where mythical creatures helped people make sense of the world. In Mesopotamia, dragons symbolized chaos and were associated with the primordial sea goddess Tiamat, representing the struggle between order and disorder. This theme continued into the medieval European dragon legends.

In Egypt, the Sphinx was linked to the sun god Ra and represented a combination of human intelligence and animal strength, guarding the secrets of the afterlife. Greek mythology featured the Chimera, a monster that embodied fear and unnatural forces, reminding societies of the fragile boundary between nature and chaos.

The Leviathan, a giant sea monster mentioned in the Bible, symbolizes the chaos of the sea. Meanwhile, griffins in Greek culture were viewed as divine guardians. As ancient myths evolved into regional folklore, they adapted to local cultures. For example, Norse sea monsters transformed into the Kraken, while dragon myths from Asia varied, with China portraying dragons as benevolent and Japan depicting them as evil serpents.

Today, the influence of these legends remains strong. Dragon myths in Europe and China continue to captivate people, representing power and luck. These ancient stories shape modern beliefs about cryptids, linking the past with the present and inspiring curiosity about the unknown.

The Thunderbird

1.2 THE ROLE OF FOLKLORE IN CRYPTID NARRATIVES

Folklore is an ancient way for stories about cryptids to be shared through time. These oral traditions form the backbone of the narrative in many societies, where the spoken word preserves the wisdom of the past and stirs the imaginations of the present. In West African cultures, griots—esteemed storytellers and custodians of history—play a pivotal role in maintaining the oral tradition. They pass on tales of mythical creatures and ancestral spirits, teaching lessons and cultural values. Their narratives entertain and educate, ensuring that the essence of these cryptid stories remains intact across generations. Similarly, Native American tribes have long shared stories of the Thunderbird. This potent spirit controls the elements, embodying their deep connection to the natural world. The Thunderbird's story, as passed down through oral tradition, serves as a reminder of the tribes' reverence for nature and its mysteries. Each retelling reinforces these beliefs, cementing the Thunderbird's place in the cultural consciousness.

. . .

Folklore shows common themes and characters that connect different cultures. One key character is the trickster, such as the Pukwudgie from Native American stories. These small, playful beings often trick humans, representing nature's unpredictability. The trickster highlights the balance of life, where humor and danger exist together. Another common theme is protective spirits, like the Scottish kelpies, which live in lakes and rivers. While these water horses can be beautiful, they fiercely protect their homes and warn of dangers hidden below the water's surface. Through these themes, folklore teaches important lessons about the relationship between humans and nature.

Folklore also reveals a culture's values and beliefs. In Japan, stories of yokai—supernatural beings—often carry moral lessons. These tales in art and literature teach people about ethical behavior and social norms. For example, the story of the Kappa, a mischievous water creature, warns children not to wander near water alone. Such stories help reinforce community values and provide moral guidance. Similarly, tales like Baba Yaga in Slavic folklore or the Banshee in Irish stories teach children to be careful and respect the world around them.

Keeping cryptid legends alive through folklore helps these stories stay relevant today. Modern versions of the Loch Ness Monster show how folklore can adapt to new formats and audiences. People remain fascinated by this famous creature from Scottish legend, which continues to capture interest through books, movies, and digital media. Each new version adds to the story and reflects society's interests and fears. Likewise, urban legends like the Slide Rock Bolter from Colorado use folklore to create modern myths that connect with local people. These stories link the past to present-day concerns about nature and technology, showing how folklore shapes and reflects cultural identity.

Humbaba from The Epic of Gilgamesh

1.3 CRYPTIDS IN HISTORICAL TEXTS AND ARTIFACTS

Cryptids have fascinated people for centuries. One of humanity's oldest texts, The Epic of Gilgamesh, introduces us to mysterious beings such as Humbaba, who guarded the Cedar Forest. Humbaba's frightening looks and magical powers show us how humans create myths to explain the unknown dangers outside their communities. Similarly, a Roman naturalist, Pliny the Elder, wrote about fantastical creatures in his work Natural History. He described dog-headed people, giant ants, and other bizarre beings, blending observation with imagination. These writings recorded known creatures and explored the possibility of undiscovered ones.

Artifacts and fossils have also fueled cryptid stories, often mixing facts with fiction. In ancient Greece, large bones, likely from mammoths or mastodons, led to the myth of the cyclopes—giant one-eyed beings. Farmers and travelers found these bones and turned them into legends. The Roc, a giant bird from Middle Eastern tales, was likely inspired by fossilized remains of ancient birds or reptiles. These discoveries highlight how humans tell stories based on the remnants of the past, blending myth with history.

Explorers and naturalists have played a key role in sharing cryptid tales. Marco Polo, a Venetian merchant, famously wrote about unicorns during his travels, but he likely meant rhinoceroses. His stories and those of other explorers captivated European audiences and sparked curiosity. In his travel accounts, Sir John Mandeville also described strange lands filled with monstrous creatures, mixing reality with imagination. These explorers expanded our understanding of cryptids, blending their observations with exotic tales.

Historical accounts have greatly influenced beliefs about cryptids. Medieval bestiaries (descriptive works on animals) mixed real and mythical animals and relied on ancient texts. These bestiaries, filled with rich illustrations, shaped how Europeans viewed the natural world and combined scientific inquiry with moral lessons. They helped people understand their environment, often giving symbolic meanings to the creatures described. Early scientific works tried to be rigorous but sometimes reinforced myths by including them in their studies. This mix of belief and skepticism continues to shape how we study cryptids.

Overall, these historical sources show that cryptids are more than just old stories; they reflect our desire to explain the unexplainable. They highlight our need to make sense of chaos and find wonder in the unknown. These ancient accounts, artifacts, and tales remind us that human imagination is diverse and boundless. These stories show how history, myth, and the quest for discovery come together.

The Werewolf

1.4 THE EVOLUTION OF CRYPTID STORIES OVER TIME

Cryptid stories have transformed over the centuries like the creatures they describe. These changes reflect the beliefs and technologies of each era. For example, werewolf legends provide an interesting look at this evolution. In medieval Europe, people linked werewolf tales to fears about witchcraft and devilry. They often portrayed werewolves as cursed humans who turned into dangerous beasts under the full moon, symbolizing the struggle within humans. As society progressed, views on werewolves also changed. Modern literature and media show them in a more complex and nuanced way, dealing with themes like identity and inner conflict. Today, werewolves are as much a part of popular culture as they are of folklore, appearing in movies and books and reflecting our current fears and interests.

Similarly, stories about sea serpents have evolved from Viking sagas to modern sightings. Vikings told tales of Jörmungandr, a giant serpent that encircled the earth, representing chaos and danger. These sea monster stories started as warnings about the ocean's dangers. As time passed and explorers traveled the seas, sailors reported seeing massive creatures in the water, adding to the legends. In modern times, these stories inspired figures like the Loch Ness Monster, which captures the mystery of the deep sea.

The 20th century brought new ways to share these stories through photography and film. Movies like "The Creature from the Black Lagoon" introduced more people to aquatic cryptid legends, mixing horror and fascination. These films are often built on old folklore, making these tales more enjoyable and accessible to a broader audience. H.P. Lovecraft's work also helped popularize cryptids by combining them with themes of deep fear and the unknown. Lovecraft depicted these creatures as part of ancient mysteries, showing our limits of understanding. This blending of literature and mythology keeps cryptid stories alive and evolving.

Technology has been important in shaping modern cryptid stories. For instance, CGI in films creates more realistic and engaging images of cryptids. This advancement allows filmmakers to bring these mythical creatures to life in new ways. Social media also plays a huge role in spreading cryptid stories. Platforms like Twitter and Reddit make it easy to share sightings and experiences quickly, encouraging discussion. This open sharing of stories helps create a global community of fans and skeptics.

Cryptid narratives are likely to keep evolving. Virtual reality could offer new experiences, letting people feel the excitement of exploring places like Loch Ness or searching for Sasquatch firsthand from the comfort of their homes. This technology could change how we interact with these stories, mixing real and imagined worlds. As cultures connect and share their own cryptid tales, these stories become symbols of our shared curiosity about the unknown.

In summary, cryptid stories are not just old tales but dynamic narratives that keep changing and thriving. Each new telling brings fresh life to these legends, helping them remain part of our culture. These stories connect to our desires to understand the world and our fears, showing the ongoing relationship between reality and imagination.

TWO
THE SCIENCE OF CRYPTIDS

Uncharted territory in the Amazon rainforest

IMAGINE STANDING at the edge of an uncharted forest, the air heavy with the scent of damp earth and the distant calls of unknown creatures. This is the threshold where cryptozoology begins, a field straddling the line between science and the unexplored mysteries of our world. Cryptozoology investigates creatures whose existence is unproven, seeking to uncover the truth behind folklore and legends. Bernard Heuvelmans, often considered the father of cryptozoology, coined the term in 1955. He approached these investigations with a blend of scientific rigor and open-mindedness, believing that the world still held secrets waiting to be discovered. Alongside Heuvelmans, Ivan T. Sanderson contributed significantly to the field, embracing the idea that not all creatures of myth were mere fabrications. Their work laid the foundation for a discipline that continues to intrigue and divide.

Trail cameras are an excellent and non-invasive research tool

2.1 CRYPTOZOOLOGY: SCIENCE OR PSEUDOSCIENCE?

Cryptozoology's relationship with mainstream science has always been complex. Unlike traditional zoology, which relies on concrete evidence and peer-reviewed studies, cryptozoology often begins with anecdotal evidence and eyewitness reports. Field investigations are a cornerstone of this discipline, where researchers venture into remote areas armed with cameras, tape recorders, plaster for footprint casts, and an array of technological tools designed to capture evidence. Trail cameras, for instance, have become invaluable, providing a way to observe wildlife without human interference. Some devices have captured images that spark discussions about mysterious figures in forests and unknown creatures in lakes. These tools show innovative ways to explore the unknown but also reveal difficulties in confirming what they find. Many scientists are skeptical about cryptozoology, as it often lacks strict methods and relies heavily on stories instead of solid evidence, making it difficult to verify.

· · ·

Critics argue that because cryptozoology has not provided verifiable proof, it loses credibility. The lack of peer-reviewed studies and the dependence on eyewitness accounts, which can be inaccurate and subjective, add to this doubt. Anecdotal evidence can be engaging but doesn't meet scientific standards for reliability. Human memory and perception can be flawed, which creates significant challenges. However, cryptozoologists argue that traditional science has sometimes overlooked evidence that later proved true; many creatures once thought to be myths were eventually accepted by science.

Cryptozoology has seen some notable successes that show its potential value. The giant squid is one such example. Once considered a myth, the giant squid was confirmed to exist through ongoing exploration and improved technology. Specimens began washing up on shores worldwide in the 1870's and 1880's. In 2004, a nearly complete specimen was caught by a fisherman trawling in the Falkland Islands and preserved at the Natural History Museum in London. Also in 2004, the first giant squid was photographed alive off the Ogasawara Islands south of Japan 900 meters deep by zoologist Dr. Tsunemi Kubodera and Kyoichi Mori. In 2012, the ability to send a specialized video system 700 meters deep into the Ogasawara archipelago allowed Dr. Kubodera and deep-sea explorer Edith Widder to film the first live video of the giant squid. Scientists had face-to-face encounters with the giant squid in their submersible a week later, taking still photos of it feeding on bait.

Similarly, the Okapi was once considered the legendary African Unicorn in the Ituri Rainforest of the Congo. Locals and explorers thought it was part giraffe, part horse, and part zebra. In 1901, Sir Harry Johnston confirmed its existence. We now identify the Okapi, which has the head and neck of a giraffe but otherwise looks like a brown-bodied zebra with stripes on its rear end and legs, as a relative of the giraffe. Its initial status as a supposed cryptid highlights the thin line between myth and reality, proving that unknown creatures can exist. However, cryptozoology has failed in other cases, such as the search for the Tasmanian Tiger. Despite many reported sightings, thorough investigations have not found evidence of its survival, highlighting the difficulties in proving the existence of cryptids.

. . .

Even though many dismiss cryptozoology as pseudoscience, it encourages curiosity and challenges what we think we know. It invites us to think about truths that might be hidden. As technology improves, so do the methods cryptozoologists use, leading to new opportunities for discovery. Despite ongoing doubts, the potential of this field to reveal hidden aspects of our world remains clear. As you stand at the edge of the forest, think about the possibility that the shadows might hide truths waiting to be uncovered, encouraging us to look beyond what we know into the mysteries that lie ahead.

The Okapi

The Amazon rainforest

2.2 ECOLOGICAL NICHES: COULD CRYPTIDS EXIST?

Ecological niches are essential for supporting biodiversity. Each species has its role within an ecosystem. These niches are shaped by specific environmental conditions and resources, allowing organisms to thrive and reduce competition. Think of a niche as nature's plan for survival, determining where and how a species lives.

The Amazon rainforest, for example, is home to countless undiscovered species that occupy hidden niches. These remote areas are full of life and may even hold cryptids—creatures some claim to exist but have never been scientifically proven. Climate, vegetation, and prey availability create conditions where unknown animals can survive, often avoiding detection because of the dense and complex environment.

Dense rainforests like those in the Amazon and Congo are prime candidates for potential cryptid habitats. These regions are full of thick tree canopies and tangled plants, making exploring difficult. In these places, species can evolve in isolation, adapting in unique ways that differ from known organisms. With its complex waterways and vast greenery, the Amazon supports a wide range of life, much of which is still unexplored. The Congo Basin is similarly rich in biodiversity and likely houses yet-to-be-discovered species. With their vast and inaccessible territories, these jungles could easily hide cryptids, providing them with the necessary resources to exist and evade discovery.

The deep ocean trenches also hold potential for cryptids. These dark, high-pressure ocean areas are among the least explored on Earth. Despite their harsh conditions, they are home to many life forms that are not yet fully understood. Creatures in these depths often have special adaptations, like bioluminescence or unique ways of feeding, to survive in such extreme environments. Like the dense forests, the ocean depths remain largely uncharted, suggesting that cryptids could also dwell in these shadows.

However, finding cryptids in these niches is challenging. Many potential habitats are in remote and rugged locations. Thick jungles and rough terrains can stop even the most dedicated explorers. Current exploration technology is advanced but still limited. While satellite images and drones can provide some information, they cannot offer the detailed insights needed for thorough studies. Investigating deep waters is complicated by weather and technical issues. These challenges and the enormity of the task make it hard to explore potential cryptid habitats properly.

The possibility of cryptids existing becomes more believable when we consider ecological principles. Cryptid-like creatures have been in the fossil record, hinting that the ancestors of today's myths once lived on Earth. The coelacanth, for example, is a fish thought to be extinct for millions of years, only to be found alive in the 20th century. Such discoveries show that we still have much to learn, and other cryptids might be hidden in ecological niches that help them survive.

Ecological niches are crucial for species adaptation and survival. They offer a stable environment and resources, allowing organisms to exploit specific conditions. This can lead to the evolution of new species. This relationship between ecological niches and species survival highlights the possibility of cryptids existing within these frameworks. As science moves forward, exploring these areas could lead to new findings that challenge our understanding of biodiversity. For now, the mystery of cryptids continues to spark our imagination and invites us to explore the hidden wonders of our world.

A two-headed snake, a rare genetic mutation caused by
incomplete splitting of an embryo

2.3 GENETIC ANOMALIES AND CRYPTID THEORIES

Occasionally, unexpected twists of nature give rise to creatures that defy
our understanding. Genetic mutations and anomalies can manifest in
extraordinary ways, leading to unusual traits or even new species.
Consider the phenomenon of polycephaly, where a single organism, such
as a snake, is born with multiple heads. This rare condition, often seen as a
biological curiosity, has fueled mythological interpretations throughout
history, painting these creatures as harbingers or divine beings. In contemporary times, occasionally, frogs develop extra legs, likely due to a parasitic flatworm. Such occurrences challenge our perception of normalcy,
suggesting that nature's creativity knows no bounds.

Another striking example is albinism, a genetic trait resulting in the
absence of pigment. In mammals, albinism can be associated with other
anomalies, such as deafness, vision problems, sunburns, and skin cancer.
In the wild, albino animals stand out against their natural surroundings,

leading animals to succumb to predators. Regarding cryptids, albinism can sometimes lead to sightings that spark legends. These genetic anomalies remind us that nature often functions beyond our known boundaries.

The role of genetics in cryptid legends is significant and should not be ignored. Genetic anomalies might provide a scientific basis for cryptid sightings, offering explanations rooted in biology rather than fantasy. For instance, the "mutant bear" theory is a possible explanation for Bigfoot sightings. In this scenario, genetic variations could result in bears with unusual physical traits, such as elongated limbs or unique fur patterns, leading eyewitnesses to mistake them for something far more mysterious. Similarly, genetic variations in large cats could contribute to reports of cryptids like the Beast of Bodmin Moor in the UK. Such cases highlight the intersection of genetics and folklore, where the extraordinary becomes plausible through the lens of scientific inquiry.

Investigating reported phenomena with a genetic basis unveils fascinating possibilities. The Loch Ness Monster, affectionately known as Nessie, has long been a subject of speculation. Some researchers propose that genetic diversity in the Loch Ness area could support the existence of a unique aquatic species hidden beneath the loch's murky depths. This genetic variability may help explain the sporadic and elusive nature of sightings of Nessie. Another intriguing aspect of genetics in cryptid reports is the potential influence of gigantism. This condition, characterized by excessive growth, could explain sightings of unusually large animals that defy common expectations. Gigantism, while rare, offers a plausible framework for understanding reports of oversized creatures lurking in the wild. Although I couldn't find good examples of this phenomenon, I did see examples of another fascinating concept: island gigantism, also called insular gigantism.

Island gigantism occurs when animals on an island increase in size dramatically in comparison to their mainland relatives. The basic theory is that in the presence of ample resources, while isolated from predators, herbivores, amphibians, and other potential prey animals evolve to become larger over time. Conversely, on an island without abundant prey available, predators, typically birds, evolve to become smaller over time.

Some very large island animals may inspire legends due to their terrifying and deadly nature; the Komodo dragon is a perfect example.

The Komodo dragon is an enormous, venomous lizard that can grow up to 10.3 feet in length and weigh up to 300 pounds. It is native to a few Indonesian islands and is currently endangered. When young, it eats small lizards, insects, and birds, but its prey gets larger until, as an adult, it can bring down a water buffalo. It can swim between islands in strong currents and run up to 13 miles per hour. Its toxic and venomous bite will slowly kill its prey over several days. With a real animal like that, who needs to concoct a legend? However, one can see how a legend might develop when explorers first saw this animal, and nothing was known about it.

Scientific research on genetics and cryptids gradually sheds light on these enigmatic beings. Advances in genetic analysis have opened new avenues for discovering previously unknown species. By examining genetic material, scientists can uncover clues about an organism's lineage, adaptations, and ecological niche. DNA evidence is crucial in cryptid investigations, offering a tangible link between legend and reality. However, interpreting this evidence requires caution. For instance, when studying Sasquatch, researchers must distinguish between mitochondrial DNA, which is inherited maternally, and nuclear DNA, which provides a broader genetic picture. This distinction is vital to avoid misinterpretation, ensuring the data accurately reflects the animal being studied.

Considering the interplay of genetics and cryptids, we find ourselves at the crossroads of science and imagination. Genetic anomalies challenge our understanding of biological norms, inviting us to explore the boundaries of what is possible. In the realm of cryptids, genetics provides a foundation for unraveling the mysteries that have captured human curiosity for generations. While the path to discovery is fraught with challenges, the potential for new revelations beckons. As we continue to probe the genetic underpinnings of cryptid legends, we may find that the truth is stranger—and more amazing—than fiction.

The Komodo Dragon

Charles Darwin's seminal work On the Origin of Species

2.4 THE ROLE OF EVOLUTION IN CRYPTID LEGENDS

Evolution is a cornerstone of biological science, a framework through which we understand the diversity of life on Earth. Charles Darwin's theory of natural selection, introduced in the 19th century, revolutionized our perception of species development. According to this theory, individuals with traits better suited to their environment are more likely to survive and reproduce. Over generations, these advantageous traits become prevalent within a population, leading to the evolution of new species. This process is not static; it involves a dynamic interplay between organisms and their environments, often described as an evolutionary arms race. Here, species continuously adapt in response to each other, driving the development of new adaptations and, sometimes, entirely new species. These principles of evolution potentially explain the existence of cryptids within nature's complexity.

Consider the concept of island gigantism, where species isolated on islands evolve larger body sizes compared to their mainland relatives. This phenomenon occurs when the absence of predators and competition allows for the growth of larger individuals, a trait that may enhance survival. Such conditions could give rise to cryptids like Bigfoot, whose purported size suggests a niche environment where gigantism is advantageous. Similarly, convergent evolution could lead to the development of cryptids with similar traits across different regions. This process occurs when unrelated species evolve similar adaptations in response to comparable environmental pressures. For example, the elongated necks of the Loch Ness Monster and other lake-dwelling cryptids might arise independently in different aquatic habitats, driven by similar ecological demands.

Some cryptids may be viewed as evolutionary relics, remnants of ancient species that have persisted into the modern age. The coelacanth, often cited as a "living fossil," exemplifies this concept. Once thought extinct, this deep-sea fish was discovered alive in the 20th century, demonstrating that species can endure in isolated environments, essentially unchanged for millions of years. This discovery fuels speculation that other cryptids, such as the Mokele-Mbembe of the Congo Basin, might be surviving dinosaur-like creatures. These legends suggest the existence of large, reptilian animals similar to sauropods, potentially lurking in the dense jungles. While intriguing, these theories require investigation as they challenge our current understanding of species survival and adaptation.

The scientific basis for theories about the existence of cryptids relies on several key factors. Although the fossil record is extensive, it has gaps that make it possible to speculate about undiscovered species. These gaps suggest that some creatures might have lived without leaving fossils. Still, the lack of fossil evidence complicates our understanding of how these cryptids might be related to known species. Proving these connections requires careful analysis and often remains uncertain without solid evidence. The scientific community seeks strong data to support claims about living fossils or unknown species, emphasizing the need for more research.

As we dive into the evolution of cryptids, we need to balance scientific study with open-minded exploration. Evolutionary theory provides a way to think about the existence of these mysterious creatures. Still, we must carefully separate realistic possibilities from fantasy. This chapter explored how evolution and cryptids intersect, focusing on how natural selection and adaptation might explain the fascinating legends. In the next chapter, we'll examine the mysteries of North America, where tales of hidden creatures continue to spark curiosity and debate.

THREE
NORTH AMERICAN MYSTERIES

Bigfoot or Sasquatch

IN THE QUIET, misty woods of North America, where the towering pines whisper secrets to the wind, an age-old mystery continues to captivate the imaginations of locals and visitors alike. This is the land of Bigfoot, a creature that has eluded definitive discovery yet continues to captivate the folklore and everyday conversations of many. The legend of Bigfoot, also called Sasquatch, evokes a deep sense of curiosity and a primal connection to the wild, untamed aspects of our world. It is a mystery that spans generations, encouraging both young and old to contemplate the possibility of the unknown.

Sasquatch in a Pacific Northwest forest

3.1 BIGFOOT: THE QUEST FOR SASQUATCH

The history of Bigfoot sightings spans decades, with notable cases that have etched themselves into the annals of cryptid lore. One of the most famous pieces of evidence is the 1967 Patterson-Gimlin film, which captured a large, dark, hairy, bipedal figure striding through the woods of Bluff Creek, California. Skeptics, believers, and scientists have scrutinized this footage, and each frame was analyzed to uncover the truth behind the figure's lumbering gait and distinctive form. Another compelling piece of evidence is the Skookum cast found in 2000 in Washington State, an impression left in the mud of what some scientists believe to be a Bigfoot's body. While this cast has fueled debates, it remains controversial, with interpretations ranging from a simple animal resting spot to the imprint of an unknown creature. Yet long before these modern encounters, Native American tribes in the Pacific Northwest told stories of Sasquatch, or Dzoonakwa (a First Nations name), a mythical giant hairy man or woman. These stories, preserved in art, totem poles, and dance, speak of a creature that had walked these lands long before settlers arrived, a testament to its deeply rooted presence in the cultural landscape. Many of the stories are warning stories, particularly to children, to behave properly so she doesn't take them away.

Over the years, Bigfoot has permeated popular culture, symbolizing the unexplained. Festivals celebrating the creature draw crowds eager to share stories, purchase memorabilia, and catch a glimpse of the legendary beast. Documentaries and movies have further cemented Bigfoot's place in the public consciousness, with each new release reigniting interest and debate. Shows like "Finding Bigfoot" and films like "Harry and the Hendersons" have introduced Bigfoot to audiences worldwide, transforming it into a cultural icon. This widespread fascination speaks to a deeper human desire to connect with mysteries that defy easy explanation, inviting us to ponder what lies beyond the edges of our understanding.

The scientific approaches to Bigfoot research are varied and innovative, employing everything from traditional footprint casts to advanced DNA analysis. Researchers meticulously study casts of footprints and hand-prints, measuring size, depth, and stride patterns and analyzing anomalies that suggest a creature unlike any known species. Though eventually debunked due to issues with mitochondrial vs. nuclear DNA, Dr. Melba Ketchum's DNA research exemplifies the efforts of interested scientists to collect and process evidence. Acoustic analysis has also emerged as a tool in the hunt for Bigfoot. The "Sierra Sounds," recorded in the high Sierra wilderness in 1972, are believed by some to capture genuine Sasquatch vocalizations. These recordings, studied by cryptolinguist R. Scott Nelson, suggest a complex language. Many people have reported hearing mutter-ings in the woods, and these have often been described as being too unin-telligible to distinguish as words. Still, they sound like language and like a conversation. Many people have also reported hearing clear words such as "hey" called out, and sometimes even their names, particularly when living in an area where they reported repeated Sasquatch sightings on their property.

Although trail cameras have become hugely popular and commonly used among Bigfoot seekers and hunters, they rarely capture images of Bigfoot, leading researchers to feel that the creature is adept at avoiding human technology. Sasquatch researchers use thermal imaging cameras at night and have often shown positive images of large creatures suspected to be Bigfoot.

Skepticism surrounding Bigfoot's existence persists, fueled by a lack of concrete physical evidence. Hoaxes have undeniably undermined credible research, casting doubt even on legitimate findings. The infamous 2002 Bigfoot costume hoax, where a man admitted to staging sightings, exemplifies the challenges researchers face. Critics highlight the lack of conclusive evidence, such as bones or bodies, as a significant obstacle despite numerous reports. Yet, the sheer volume of eyewitness encounters is impossible to ignore. Thousands of reports detail encounters with a large hairy bipedal creature deep in the forest, where broken trees, thrown rocks, and stolen food suggest the presence of an intelligent, elusive, and sometimes terrifying being. Podcasts such as "Sasquatch Chronicles" and "Bigfoot and Beyond," along with YouTube channels focused on Bigfoot encounters, provide platforms for witnesses to share their stories, contributing to the fascinating collection of Sasquatch lore that continues to captivate and fascinate many people.

Check out social media for all kinds of information on Sasquatch sightings from all over the United States. Listen to podcasts for intense eyewitness stories that are hard to discredit. See my book Sasquatch: Insights into Their Lives and Encounters with Humans for a compilation of Sasquatch actions from over a thousand eyewitness reports.

The Mothman

3.2 MOTHMAN: WEST VIRGINIA'S WINGED ENIGMA

In the mid-1960s, Point Pleasant, West Virginia, became the center of strange events that changed the town forever. On a cold November night in 1966, two young couples driving near the TNT plant, an abandoned World War II munitions site, saw a creature that was hard to explain. They described it as a large gray figure with wings folded around its body and glowing red eyes that seemed to pierce right through the darkness. The creature followed them as they quickly drove away, screeching and moving easily at high speed, and rising like a helicopter. This sighting was just the start. Over the next year, many people reported seeing a similar entity, adding to the growing legend of the Mothman. The creature's frightening presence seemed connected to the tragic collapse of the Silver Bridge in December 1967, which killed 46 people, as it had been seen in the area before the collapse, which had left the town in shock. To many, Mothman was not just a mysterious visitor but also a harbinger of disaster, linking it forever to this tragedy. The Mothman sightings and the subsequent bridge collapse had a profound psychological and cultural impact on the people of Point Pleasant.

. . .

The Mothman sightings caused real worry and concern in some Point Pleasant residents. Eyewitnesses reported feeling dread as if the creature's presence meant something terrible was about to happen. Interviews with those who saw Mothman showed a wide range of emotions, from fear and anxiety to a strange sense of impending doom. The psychological impact of the Mothman sightings on the witnesses provides a more comprehensive understanding of the legend's effects, highlighting the fear and fascination it instilled in the local community.

Many theories exist about Mothman's nature and origins, ranging from simple explanations to the supernatural. Some think the creature is just a misidentified sandhill crane, a bird native to the area that can look otherworldly in the dark. Others believe Mothman may have come from another realm, possibly linked to UFO sightings around the same time. Paranormal opinions often view Mothman as an interdimensional being beyond human understanding. While these ideas are speculative, they show our desire to find explanations for strange happenings, mixing science with fantasy.

Mothman's legacy remains strong, woven into the culture of Point Pleasant and beyond. The annual Mothman Festival celebrates this mysterious figure, attracting thousands of visitors from afar. The festival features guest speakers, tours of the area, and Mothman-themed merchandise, transforming a once-feared creature into a beloved icon. "The Mothman Prophecies," a book by John Keel, further established Mothman's place in pop culture. Its 2002 movie adaptation brought the legend to more people, blending fact and fiction into an engaging story. Through these cultural events, Mothman has moved beyond its origins, becoming a symbol of the unknown and showing the lasting power of folklore.

Mothman sightings still occur, particularly around the Chicago, IL area. A sighting occurred in Kane County, IL in April, 2024. A truck driver saw a 12-foot humanoid, brown furry creature with arms, legs, and wings flying along after his vehicle. This was his third sighting, the first two being 10 miles away and three weeks apart, the previous year. As it swooped down at his vehicle, nearly covering his windshield, he was afraid for his life and began shooting at it. It wrapped itself in its wings, started descending, and was gone.

Short videos can occasionally be found on TikTok and YouTube. If you decide to check out any of these reports, see what you think and make your own assessment.

The Dogman

3.3 DOGMAN: TERROR ON TWO LEGS

The legend of the Dogman finds its roots in the dense forests of Michigan, where it first emerged in the late 19th century; thus, it is often referred to as the Michigan Dogman. In 1887, Wexford County was the site of a chilling encounter that would ignite local folklore. Two lumberjacks claimed to have seen a creature that defied categorization, half-dog, half-man, prowling the woods. This sighting was not an isolated incident. It tapped into a rich tapestry of Native American legends and early settler tales, where wolf-like creatures roamed the forests under the cover of night. These stories, passed down through generations, spoke of supernatural beings capable of shifting shapes, blending the line between man and beast. The Dogman legend grew, weaving itself into the region's cultural fabric, a terrifying presence lurking just beyond the reach of civilization.

The origins of the Dogman are unclear, and many theories exist. Some think it might be a large wolf or bear seen in dim light. Others believe it could be a rare genetic mutation that creates its unusual features. Many view the Dogman as a paranormal being, like the werewolves of Europe or the skinwalkers from Native American legends. These beings are said to change shape and take on the form of animals. The legends illustrate a profound fear of the unknown, intertwining humans and animals into a mysterious tale.

Reports of the Dogman have appeared across the U.S., from the forests of Wisconsin to the deserts of the Southwest, with each story adding to its legend. Dogman sightings also occur outside the United States, with reports in Mexico and Canada. These accounts suggest a more widely distributed creature or legend. In Mexico, stories of the Nahual, a shape-shifting figure from Aztec mythology, mirror Dogman legends, pointing to a shared cultural theme. Although Canadian sightings are less frequent, they share similarities with U.S. reports describing an elusive and frightening creature. These encounters often come with strange howls and unexplained tracks, leaving an unforgettable impression on those who experience them. The Dogman remains a terrifying figure that continues to haunt our imagination.

Eyewitness accounts of Dogmen encounters vary widely. Witnesses often describe them as creatures over seven feet tall, standing upright with a man's body and the head of a wolf or dog. They usually have upright, pointed ears and a long shepherd-like nose. Their hind legs are "pointy" like a dog's typically are but are more muscular and strangely hold the creature upright. Some are described as having spindlier front legs and front paws, more like raccoon hands. Their eyes seem to glow in the dark and can be seen from far away through the night. I have listened to dozens of Dogman encounters on podcasts, which are terrifying. Typically, the creatures are aggressive, stalking or chasing people. They seem to appear from out of nowhere, from out of forests or down embankments or across fields. They have been reported to growl at people and their car windows, drool and snarl at their cars and windows, claw, scrape, and bang on cars, and chase after them.

You can listen to many Dogman encounters on the podcast Sasquatch Chronicles with Wes Gerber. Dogman sightings can be found on TikTok and YouTube. I saw one video of a strange dog-like creature approaching people in their car and looking very threateningly in the window, which was pretty creepy. Many of the videos and webcam images appear to look like wolves and dogs. Check it out and see what you think.

The Jersey Devil

3.4 THE JERSEY DEVIL: FACT OR FOLKLORE?

In the heart of New Jersey's Pine Barrens, a dense and mysterious forest, the legend of the Jersey Devil has taken root, thriving for over 250 years. The origins of this tale trace back to the early 18th century, centered around the Leeds family, whose matriarch, Mother Leeds, is said to have cursed her unwanted thirteenth child. Because of the curse, upon its birth, the child reportedly transformed into a creature with leathery wings, a horse's head, and a forked tail before flying up the chimney and into the surrounding woods. The Jersey Devil is a legend that began in colonial America, fueled by local superstitions and fears. This story features the creature that terrorizes the area and links back to the Leeds family. Many reports describe the Jersey Devil as a creature that causes livestock deaths and makes eerie sounds at night, becoming a part of local culture.

In 1909, the Jersey Devil became widely known during a week of panic when hundreds claimed they saw the creature. Newspapers reported sightings detailing the beast's frightening looks and alleged attacks, which caused schools and factories to close due to fear. These sensational stories captured the public's attention and helped solidify the Jersey Devil's place in folklore. Over the years, people have continued to report sightings, ranging from quick glimpses to more serious encounters where the creature allegedly threatened people. While details vary, these stories consistently describe a fantastical creature, perpetuating its reputation as a local threat and a fascinating mystery.

The Jersey Devil symbolizes the fears and identity of the region. It represents the wild and unpredictable nature of the Pine Barrens, a large and often misunderstood area. This connection to the land makes the Jersey Devil an essential part of local folklore, reminding people of the untamed nature near settled areas. The legend has even influenced local culture, as seen in the NHL's New Jersey Devils hockey team, which uses the legend as part of its identity. This shows how the creature has become a source of pride and interest for locals.

Despite its legendary status, many people question the existence of the Jersey Devil. Some suggest that reported sightings are simply cases of mistaken identity, where animals like cranes or deer are mistaken for the creature, especially in low visibility. Skeptics argue that the story lacks proof and is too strange to be true. Nevertheless, some eyewitnesses provide photos or videos showing the creature. One person claimed to see the Jersey Devil in a tree, and the image gained notoriety online. Another report came from a father and son who spotted the creature while hiking, their detailed descriptions adding to the collection of firsthand accounts. While many dismiss these stories, they keep the legend alive, making the Jersey Devil an enduring symbol of the unknown.

Check online for videos and firsthand accounts and make your own assessment. Is the Jersey Devil real or not?

The Skunk Ape

3.5 CHASING THE SKUNK APE: FLORIDA'S MYTHICAL PRIMATE

In the sweltering heat of Florida's Everglades, a creature roams that has sparked intrigue and fear. Known as the Skunk Ape, this elusive being is said to resemble a large, foul-smelling primate. Its legend weaves through the fabric of Florida's folklore, becoming as much a part of the landscape as the alligators and cypress trees. Notable sightings have been reported throughout the Everglades and its surrounding areas, with witnesses describing a creature that moves with surprising agility despite its formidable size. These accounts often speak of an overwhelming stench, reminiscent of rotting vegetation, that lingers long after the creature has vanished into the dense foliage. The Skunk Ape has become a symbol of local mystery, drawing tourists eager to catch a glimpse of this Floridian legend or to hear the stories that have captivated generations. It has also inspired a cottage industry of tours and merchandise, feeding a cultural fascination with the unknown.

. . .

Evidence of the Skunk Ape's existence is as varied as the stories themselves. One of the most famous pieces of evidence is the Myakka Skunk Ape photos taken by an anonymous woman in 2000. The images depict a large, apelike figure partially obscured by palmetto fronds. Critics argue these photos are inconclusive, yet they remain a focal point for believers. Footprint casts have been collected over the years, showing large, humanoid impressions that defy easy categorization. Trail cameras have occasionally captured blurry images of what some claim to be the Skunk Ape. However, skeptics point out the lack of clarity and definitive proof. Despite the controversies, these pieces of evidence continue to fuel debates and keep the legend alive.

With its rich biodiversity and sprawling wetlands, the Florida Everglades presents an ideal habitat for a creature like the Skunk Ape. This unique ecosystem is home to a myriad of species, many of which are found nowhere else on Earth. Its dense vegetation and expansive waterways create a labyrinthine landscape that is difficult to navigate, offering ample hiding spots for any creature seeking solitude. The challenges of conducting scientific research in such an environment are immense. The heat, humidity, and presence of venomous wildlife make fieldwork arduous and, at times, perilous. These conditions increase the likelihood of undiscovered species, enhancing the Skunk Ape legend's credibility.

The Skunk Ape occupies a fascinating niche within the broader context of cryptozoological studies. Often compared to Bigfoot and other North American cryptids, the Skunk Ape adds a regional twist to the myth of the hidden primate. Its presence in Florida has influenced cryptid hunting culture, leading to dedicated research groups and expeditions aimed at uncovering the truth. Enthusiasts and researchers alike are drawn to the Everglades, where they hope to document definitive evidence of the Skunk Ape. This pursuit reflects a broader human desire to explore the unknown and uncover the things that are hidden within the world's wild places.

Eyewitness encounters with the Skunk Ape are as compelling as they are varied. Residents often recount sightings that have left them both fasci-nated and unnerved. One resident described a late-night encounter where they saw the creature standing at the edge of their property, its eyes reflecting the moonlight. It reportedly let out a deep, guttural sound before retreating into the swamp, leaving the witness with a sense of awe and disbelief. Countless firsthand accounts provide a rich collection of stories that vividly depict the Skunk Ape's behaviors. From its nocturnal habits to its elusive nature, the Skunk Ape continues to captivate and challenge our understanding of what might be lurking in the shadows of the Everglades.

Visit TikTok for some compelling video footage and trail camera photos of Skunk Apes.

Read the book <u>Enoch, a Bigfoot Story</u> for a compelling narrative of an amazing eyewitness account of a Skunk Ape by the author Autumn Williams, who is herself a long-term Sasquatch eyewitness, researcher, and celebrity. I love this book for its honesty and poignancy in the delicate friendship between the person and the Skunk Ape. Whether you believe it or not, this book potentially answers many questions about the behavior of Skunk Apes.

FOUR
EUROPEAN LEGENDS

The Loch Ness Monster

. . .

THE MISTY WATERS of Loch Ness in Scotland hold a mystery that has fascinated people for generations. It is a tale that combines ancient folklore with modern curiosity, drawing visitors from around the globe to its tranquil shores. Here, nestled among the Scottish Highlands, lies the legend of the Loch Ness Monster, otherwise known as Nessie. This elusive creature's story is woven with sightings, scientific investigations, and cultural significance, making it one of the most enduring cryptid legends in the world.

Nessie swimming along Loch Ness in the morning mist.

4.1 LOCH NESS MONSTER: SCOTLAND'S ELUSIVE NESSIE

The legend of Nessie took a significant turn in 1933 when George Spicer and his wife reported seeing a large, prehistoric-looking creature cross the road in front of their car. Described as having a long neck and large body, their account captivated the public's imagination and sparked a media frenzy. This sighting marked the beginning of Nessie's modern legend, drawing attention from curious individuals and researchers alike. In 1934, the infamous "Surgeon's Photograph" emerged, supposedly capturing Nessie's head and neck protruding from the water. While this image became iconic, it was eventually revealed to be a hoax involving a toy submarine and a bit of creative trickery. Despite this revelation, the photograph solidified Nessie's place in popular culture, fueling both skepticism and belief.

Scientific endeavors to uncover the truth about Nessie have been numerous, varied, and ongoing. The 1970s saw the formation of the Loch Ness Investigation Bureau, a group dedicated to studying the loch and its mysterious inhabitants. Utilizing sonar technology, they sought to detect any large, moving objects beneath the surface. Although these efforts did not provide conclusive evidence, they laid the groundwork for future explorations. More recently, genetic studies of Loch Ness water samples were conducted, aiming to identify any unusual DNA that might hint at Nessie's presence. While no evidence of a large creature like a plesiosaur was found, the study did suggest the presence of numerous eels, leading to speculation that sightings could be attributed to oversized specimens.

Nessie is more than just a cryptid; it is integral to Scottish identity and folklore. The creature's legend has become intertwined with the region's cultural heritage. Nessie's impact on Scottish tourism is significant, drawing over a million visitors annually, each eager to explore the loch and catch a glimpse of its famous resident. Local businesses capitalize on this fascination, offering tours, souvenirs, and events centered around the legend. Nessie narratives also permeate local folklore, with stories passed down through generations, adding to the rich fabric of Scottish mythology.

Media portrayals of Nessie have played a crucial role in shaping public perception. From films and documentaries to literature and children's books, Nessie has been depicted in a myriad of ways, each adding to the creature's allure. These portrayals often blend fact and fiction, creating narratives that capture the imagination while reinforcing the mystery. The media continues to significantly impact the legend of Nessie, helping to keep it recognized around the world as a symbol of the unexplained.

Recent evidence suggests that something unusual may lurk beneath the waters of Loch Ness. In 2023, a series of 15 photos taken in 2018 were revealed, depicting a large, dark object moving through the water. These images are difficult to refute and have reignited interest in the legend. In 2024, sonar readings from a vessel detected a large creature with a long neck moving against the current, further fueling speculation. That same year, a webcam sighting captured a long, dark creature leaving a wake, and a photo taken in April showed a dark object consistent with Nessie's shape. These sightings, alongside numerous others, keep the legend alive, inviting us to ponder the mysteries that lie beneath the surface of Loch Ness.

. . .

Check out the webcams of Loch Ness at lochness.co.uk. Kudos to the efforts of so many people who made this project successful. Cryptid enthusiasts worldwide can now enjoy watching the Loch through these webcams!

Reflection Section: Personal Encounters and Beliefs

Consider your own beliefs about unexplained phenomena. Have you ever experienced or heard a story that challenged your understanding of reality and how you see the world around you? Reflect on how such encounters might shape your perception of legends like Nessie. What role do these stories play in your cultural or personal identity?

The Beast of Bodmin

4.2 THE BEAST OF BODMIN: A CORNISH CONUNDRUM

In the rolling moors of Cornwall, the legend of the Beast of Bodmin has captured the public's imagination, evolving from mere suspicion into a widely recognized phenomenon. Throughout the 1990s, reports of a mysterious large cat, often described as a phantom black panther, circulated in the media, captivating readers and sparking debates about its existence. This period saw a surge in sightings, ranging from fleeting glimpses to more detailed accounts of a creature with sharp teeth and yellow-white eyes lurking in the rugged landscape of the moors.

The media coverage during this time acted as a catalyst, transforming local folklore into a nationwide intrigue. Unverified photographs emerged, showing the silhouette of an animal that defied conventional explanation. Though these images were scrutinized for authenticity, they further fueled public interest and speculation.

. . .

Cornish folklore has long been a tapestry of myths and legends, with the Beast of Bodmin fitting seamlessly into this cultural narrative. The tales of large, mysterious cats echo ancient Celtic myths, where creatures of the wild were revered and feared in equal measure. Oral tradition plays a crucial role in preserving these stories, passed down through generations in the communal settings of the hearth and home. In these tales, the moors become a character, a wild and untamed land where the line between myth and reality blurs. This rich folklore provides a fertile ground for the Beast's legend, intertwining with historical accounts to create a compelling and elusive narrative.

In response to the growing public concern, the UK government launched an official investigation in 1995 to determine the presence of big cats on Bodmin Moor. The investigation aimed to provide clarity and address the mounting reports of sightings. Despite extensive ecological studies and searches, the findings were inconclusive. The report acknowledged the lack of verifiable evidence for a breeding population of big cats, yet it did not entirely dismiss the possibility of their presence. This ambiguity left room for continued debate, with some theories suggesting that the Beast might be an escaped exotic pet. During the 1970s and 1980s, the release of such animals from private collections was not uncommon, leading to speculation that the Beast of Bodmin could be a remnant of this era. This theory, while plausible, remains unproven.

The cultural impact of the Beast of Bodmin extends beyond the moors, influencing Cornish identity and tourism. The legend has become a part of Cornwall's allure, drawing visitors eager to explore the land where the Beast is said to roam. Local businesses have embraced the mystery, offering tours and merchandise that capitalize on the enduring fascination. Public debates continue to thrive, fueled by new sightings and media portrayals that keep the legend alive. In 1998, video footage surfaced, showing a black animal, likely a big cat, approximately 3.5 feet long. The curator of Newquay Zoo described this footage as the "best evidence yet" that big cats inhabit Bodmin Moor. The video reignited discussions and brought renewed attention to the legend, prompting believers and skeptics to reassess their views.

· · ·

Eyewitness accounts remain the backbone of the Beast's legend, providing a narrative that is as diverse as it is intriguing. Locals and visitors alike recount stories of encounters with a shadowy creature moving with a feline grace across the moors. Some describe the thrill of seeing the Beast silhouetted against the twilight sky. In contrast, others speak of a chilling presence felt rather than seen. These accounts, though subjective, contribute to the richness of the Beast's story, ensuring its place in the annals of Cornish folklore. Whether a product of myth, misidentification, or reality, the legend of the Beast of Bodmin continues to captivate those who wander the moor, searching for a glimpse of the unknown.

The Werewolf

4.3 WEREWOLVES: MYTHS OF THE MOONLIT NIGHTS

The lore of werewolves stretches back into the annals of European history, where ancient Greeks and Romans depicted tales of men transforming into wolves, embodying the raw, untamed nature that lurked beneath civilization's veneer. In Greek mythology, the story of King Lycaon is a well-known tale where Zeus transformed him into a wolf as punishment for his impiety and cannibalism. These early narratives often portrayed lycanthropy as a curse, a divine retribution that stripped an individual of their humanity. As these myths traveled through time, they evolved, adapting to the cultural and social climates they encountered. During the medieval period, the lore of werewolves gained new dimensions, deeply intertwined with the witch hunts that swept across Europe. The fear of the supernatural and the unknown gave rise to werewolf trials, where individuals were accused of transforming into wolves and committing heinous acts. Often, these accusations were leveled against marginalized members of society, creating scapegoats for unexplained tragedies or events. Confessions, frequently extracted under duress, painted vivid, terrifying pictures of transformation and savagery, further embedding the werewolf mythos into the cultural consciousness of the time.

The persistence of werewolf legends can be attributed to the psychological and societal factors that have kept these stories alive. In medieval societies, fear and superstition were pervasive. Werewolves' dual nature of man and beast became metaphors for the internal struggle between civilization and the primal instincts within us all. They challenged the thin veneer of control that society imposed on the natural world, serving as cautionary tales of what might happen if one succumbed to base desires. These myths also provided a framework for understanding human transformation and change, illustrating the potential for darkness that lies beneath the surface of every individual. This duality resonated deeply, making werewolves not just figures of fear but also symbols of transformation and the boundaries of human nature.

Scientific inquiry has sought to explain the werewolf phenomenon through various lenses, offering biological and psychological theories that provide alternative narratives of the supernatural. Hypertrichosis, characterized by excessive hair growth, has historically been associated with werewolf legends. Individuals affected by this condition, often called "werewolf syndrome," might have been perceived as living embodiments of the myth, their appearance fueling tales of transformation. Additionally, clinical lycanthropy, a rare psychiatric condition where individuals believe they can transform into animals, presents another potential explanation. This delusion, while uncommon, sheds light on the psychological underpinnings of the werewolf myth, illustrating how deeply held beliefs and fears can manifest in both the mind and society.

Werewolves have left an indelible mark on literature and media, evolving from terrifying figures in folklore to complex characters in contemporary storytelling. Early cinematic portrayals, such as the 1941 film "The Wolf Man," cemented the werewolf's place in popular culture, introducing audiences to the tragic, cursed figure of Larry Talbot. This portrayal highlighted themes of identity, control, and the monstrous within, resonating with viewers and influencing subsequent depictions. In modern fantasy literature, werewolves have experienced a resurgence, often depicted as multifaceted beings with complex social structures and moral codes. Series like "The Twilight Saga" and "The Dresden Files" explore the nuances of werewolf existence, presenting them as both allies and adversaries in the supernatural realm. These stories reflect ongoing fascinations with transformation and the boundaries of human nature.

A Pixie

4.4 IRISH LEPRECHAUNS, PIXIES, BANSHEES AND POOKA

In the rich tapestry of Irish folklore, leprechauns are one of the most enigmatic and well-loved figures. These solitary fairies, often depicted as diminutive old men clad in green, are the quintessential tricksters of Irish mythology. They are said to live in remote areas, crafting shoes and guarding their hidden pots of gold, which they might reveal if captured—though they are notorious for their cunning tricks, often escaping by convincing their captor to look away. The rainbow, a symbol of their elusive nature, is usually associated with the location of their treasure, adding a mystical element to their lore. This imagery of leprechauns guarding gold at the rainbow's end has captivated imaginations world-wide, making them symbols of luck and mischief.

Yet, leprechauns are not the only mystical beings that populate the rich world of Irish legends. Pixies, as portrayed in the AI-generated picture above, are tiny humanoids, sometimes called small fairies, with or without wings, and are called Aos Si or Aos Sidhe in Ireland. They are believed to live in ancient sites underground, such as barrows and stone circles. They are known for being playful and might help with chores, or be mischievous, leading a traveler astray. Another is the Banshee, an iconic figure, shrouded in mystery and foreboding. Known as a harbinger of death, the Banshee's mournful wail is said to foretell the passing of a family member, a chilling reminder of mortality. Her presence in Irish folklore underscores the cultural themes of death and mourning, reflecting the deep connection between the living and the spiritual realm. Then there is the Pooka, a shape-shifting trickster spirit that can take many forms, from a black horse to a sleek goat. The Pooka embodies the unpredictability of nature and the supernatural, often serving as both a helper and a hindrance to those who encounter it. These creatures, along with leprechauns, create a colorful and diverse group of mythical beings that enhance and enrich Irish tales.

The cultural significance of these creatures in Ireland is profound, reflecting and reinforcing the values and traditions of the Irish people. Folklore is crucial in preserving the Irish language and its rich oral traditions, passing down stories that connect generations. Through tales of leprechauns, the Irish celebrate resilience and humor, embodying a spirit of wit and cleverness that characterizes the national identity. Whether shared around a fire or told in stories, these myths are important to Irish culture. They help connect people to their heritage and create a familiar tale that honors both magical and everyday experiences.

In modern times, leprechauns and their fellow mythical creatures have been woven into the fabric of global popular culture, often through commercialization and media portrayals. Leprechauns are closely associated with St. Patrick's Day celebrations, where their image captures the playful spirit of the holiday. While some see this commercialization as losing original folklore, it has also helped share Irish mythology with more people, increasing appreciation for its richness. Irish folklore has influenced films, books, and art worldwide, showcasing its whimsical and fantastical elements.

A unique perspective on leprechauns and their enduring legacy comes from Kevin Wood, the sole remaining "Leprechaun whisperer" in Carlingford, County Louth, Ireland. Wood claims to have a deep connection with these mythical beings, sharing stories of encounters and insights into their world. His tales offer a rare glimpse into the living tradition of leprechaun lore, bridging the gap between ancient myth and contemporary belief. For those who wish to delve into the essence of Irish folklore, voices like Wood's offer invaluable insights that help maintain the enchantment in a world that frequently favors rationality. As the chapter concludes, the lasting appeal of these legends encourages readers to reflect on the myths that shape their own cultures, paving the way for exploring the mystical creatures found in other parts of the world.

My searches revealed compelling video sightings of Pixies online. (The same is true of fairies). This was not the case with Leprechauns. However, some Irish people interviewed online seemed earnest in believing that Leprechauns were real.

FIVE
CRYPTIDS OF ASIA

The Yeti

ENVISION AN EXPANSE of snow-covered peaks so vast, in silence so profound, and the air so thin you can barely breathe. This is the Himalayan range, where many of nature's mysteries remain. Amidst these towering giants, tales of the Yeti, also known as the "Abominable Snowman," have persisted for centuries. Described as a tall, ape-like figure with shaggy white fur, the Yeti occupies a unique place in both folklore and potential reality. Its legend is woven into the region's cultural fabric, which is particularly important to the indigenous Sherpa and Tibetan communities living in these rugged landscapes.

The Yeti

5.1 THE YETI: ASIA'S ABOMINABLE SNOWMAN

The Sherpa people believe in the Yeti and feel its presence in the mountains. Its origins are deeply rooted in the regional folklore. In their traditions, the Yeti is more than just a creature; it is a spiritual entity important to their culture. Known in the pre-Buddhist religion Bön as the "Glacier Being," the Yeti was revered as a deity, worshipped through spiritual ceremonies and even animal sacrifices. This belief system cast the Yeti as a powerful figure, embodying the untamed forces of nature in the high mountains. Sherpa legends often depict the Yeti as a guardian of the mountains, commanding respect and awe, reinforcing the spiritual bond between the people and their environment.

Tibetan tales further enrich the Yeti's mythos, portraying it as a watchful protector of the Himalayas. According to these stories, the Yeti serves as a sentinel, guarding the sacred peaks from intruders and preserving the sanctity of the land. This role as a guardian aligns with the region's spiritual views, where mountains are seen as the homes of deities and the Yeti as their earthly representative. Such narratives underscore the deep cultural ties between the Yeti and the Himalayan communities, where the creature symbolizes the awe-inspiring power and mystery of the natural world.

Documented sightings and expeditions have sought to uncover the truth behind the Yeti, blending folklore with scientific inquiry. One of the most notable pieces of evidence emerged in 1951 when mountaineer Eric Shipton photographed large footprints on the slopes of Mount Everest. These prints sparked significant interest, marking a pivotal moment in Yeti research. The footprints, measuring 13 inches in length, were unlike any known animal track, leading to more speculation about the Yeti's existence. Shipton's photographs fueled a wave of expeditions, each hoping to catch the elusive creature on camera. In his words, published in The Times, "It showed three "toes" and a broad "thumb" to the side. What was particularly interesting was that where the tracks crossed a crevasse one could see quite clearly where the creature had jumped and used its toes to secure purchase on the snow on the other side. We followed the tracks for more than a mile down the glacier before we got on to moraine-covered ice."

Renowned mountaineers Sir Edmund Hillary and Tenzing Norgay also contributed to the Yeti's legend. During their historic ascent of Everest in 1953, they encountered what they believed to be Yeti tracks. Their accounts added credibility, as both men were respected figures in the mountaineering community. These sightings and their testimonies helped make the Yeti a famous cryptid worldwide. Hillary returned to the Himalayas in 1960 with a large team and a well-funded expedition in search of the Yeti. They planned to use a dart gun to tranquilize one and examine it but never found one.

One more recent mountaineering account in the Himalayas reported that the climber found a trackway in the snow with large, human-like footprints. Upon returning the following day to show his sherpas for confirmation, his sherpas walked past it, refusing to look at the trackway and pretending it did not exist. He found this puzzling but suspected that his sherpas were afraid to acknowledge the presumably Yeti footprints for some reason, either because it was in the vicinity or because they felt that it might lend it power by acknowledging it.

In 2008, hair samples purported to be from Yeti were tested for their DNA, but bringing scientific testing to the mystery did little to solve it. The samples, collected from remote Himalayan regions, were subjected to rigorous tests, revealing genetic similarities to known bear species. This finding supported the theory that the Yeti might be a type of bear, possibly a yet-undiscovered subspecies adapted to the harsh mountain environment. However, if the Yeti is a bear, its 5-toed tracks are unlike any known bear's and very much like a humanoid creature. Despite these scientific insights, the debate over the Yeti's true identity continues, with no conclusive evidence to confirm or deny its existence.

The Yeti's influence extends beyond the mountains, permeating popular culture and global perceptions. In films and documentaries, the Yeti often appears as a formidable yet misunderstood creature, capturing the imagination of viewers worldwide. This portrayal has elevated the Yeti to a symbol of adventure and the unknown, drawing tourists to the Himalayas for their possible Yeti encounter. Adventure tourism has flourished, with trekkers hoping to glimpse the creature that has influenced storytellers for generations.

Eyewitness encounters with the Yeti are ongoing. Many adventurers have reported seeing large, bipedal figures moving swiftly across snowy landscapes, leaving behind massive footprints that defy straightforward explanation. These sightings, often accompanied by tales of unearthly howls echoing through the valleys, keep the Yeti's legend alive for those who venture into the Himalayas. The numerous tracks found in these remote regions serve as tantalizing reminders of the mysteries that endure in these majestic mountains.

The Ningen

5.2 NINGEN: THE MYSTERIOUS ANTARCTIC HUMANOID

In the icy waters surrounding Antarctica, a creature known as the Ningen stirs the imagination. Originating from the digital depths of Japanese internet forums in the mid-2000s, the legend of the Ningen quickly spread. The story begins with crew members aboard Japanese whale research ships, who reportedly witnessed large, humanoid figures gliding beneath the frigid waves. These initial sightings hinted at something extraordinary lurking in the subantarctic oceans. As these tales circulated, online communities latched onto the idea, weaving intricate narratives that blurred the lines between reality and myth. The Ningen became a sensation, its story evolving through countless retellings and digital discussions.

Descriptions of the Ningen are as varied as they are intriguing. Witnesses often describe it as a massive, pale-skinned figure with distinctly human-like features, a creature that defies precise categorization. Some accounts suggest that the Ningen resembles a colossal aquatic humanoid, its smooth skin and elongated limbs moving with an eerie grace through the water. Others depict it as a whale-like entity, its enormous size and gentle movements evoking a sense of majesty. These sightings, often shrouded in the fog and darkness of the Antarctic night, add to the Ningen's mystique, suggesting a creature that exists beyond the edges of our understanding.

Theories about the Ningen's true nature abound, offering a different perspective on this enigmatic being. One hypothesis is that the Ningen could be an undiscovered marine mammal, a species that has adapted to the harsh conditions of the southern oceans. This theory, while speculative, invites us to consider the vastness of the sea and the many secrets it still holds. Skeptics, however, argue that sightings of the Ningen can be attributed to icebergs or illusions, like an oasis in the desert. This phenomenon can easily mislead the eye in the dim light of polar regions. The interplay of light and shadow on the ice and the vastness of the Antarctic landscape can create shapes and figures that evoke the uncanny, feeding into the legend.

The Ningen's impact on Japanese pop culture has been significant, with its presence felt across various forms of media. In manga and anime, the Ningen often appears as a mysterious creature, its story woven into plots that explore themes of nature and the unknown. This representation has cemented the Ningen as a modern myth. This narrative resonates with audiences who are drawn to stories of the unexplained. The creature's eerie allure has also inspired artists and writers who use the Ningen to explore the boundaries of imagination and reality. In doing so, the Ningen has become a symbol of intrigue, a testament to the power of storytelling in shaping our perceptions of the world.

In modern Japanese folklore, the Ningen occupies a unique position, embodying the intersection of myth and digital culture. Borne from the internet's fertile ground, its story reflects how technology and storytelling can work together to create new legends that capture the public's imagination. As the Ningen continues to inspire curiosity and speculation, it stands as a reminder of things undiscovered that still lie hidden in the depths of our planet's most remote places.

The Mongolian Death Worm

5.3 THE MONGOLIAN DEATH WORM: DESERT LEGENDS

In the arid expanses of the Gobi Desert, a creature of legend slithers beneath the sands, known as the Mongolian Death Worm. Local legends describe this cryptid as a fearsome entity, capable of killing with a mere touch. It resembles a large, blood-red worm, two to five feet long and armed with a venomous spray or an electric discharge powerful enough to kill a camel. The stories have been told for generations among the nomadic tribes of Mongolia, who speak of the worm with reverence and fear. It is said to appear with the scorching heat of the desert sun, emerging from the sand like a living nightmare, ready to strike.

Despite the terror it inspires, the Death Worm's existence remains unverified. Throughout the years, various expeditions have ventured into the Gobi Desert, driven by the temptation of uncovering this elusive creature. Among the most notable were the attempts of Ivan Mackerle, a Czech cryptozoologist who led several expeditions in the 1990s. Mackerle, intrigued by the tales and determined to find evidence, employed a mix of scientific equipment and local knowledge. He and his team used seismic vibrations to mimic the movement of prey, hoping to lure the Death Worm from its sandy lairs. Though they captured fascinating footage and interviews with locals, definitive proof of the worm's existence eluded them. However, eyewitness testimonies from nomadic tribespeople continue to support the worm's presence. These accounts describe encounters with a creature that defies conventional classification.

Scientific perspectives on the Death Worm phenomenon offer explanations that ground the legend in more familiar terms. Some theories suggest that the Death Worm is a misidentified snake or lizard, possibly the Tartar sand boa, a species native to the region. With its burrowing habits and distinctive appearance, the sand boa might easily be mistaken for the mythical worm. Environmental factors also play a role in sustaining the legend. The harsh desert conditions, with their extreme temperatures and arid landscapes, can warp perceptions and give rise to fantastical stories. Mirages and the play of light on the shifting sands can create illusions, further fueling the myth of the Death Worm. These scientific explanations, while plausible, do not diminish the allure of the legend. Instead, they invite us to consider how the natural world can inspire stories that blur the line between reality and imagination.

The Mongolian Death Worm's influence extends beyond folklore, leaving a mark on Mongolian culture and tourism. In storytelling traditions, the worm symbolizes the desert's untamed power, a reminder of nature's unpredictable and often dangerous beauty. These stories, shared around campfires and passed down through generations, reinforce the cultural identity of the Mongolian people, connecting them to their land in profound ways. The legend also plays a significant role in promoting adventure tourism in the Gobi Desert. Travelers, drawn by the promise of uncovering the unknown, flock to the region in hopes of experiencing the mystique of the Death Worm firsthand. Guided tours and expeditions capitalize on this curiosity, blending cultural immersion and thrilling exploration. The legend, therefore, acts as a bridge between the past and the present, inviting both locals and visitors to explore the rich Mongolian heritage and the enigmatic wonders of the desert.

· · ·

Visit TikTok for compelling sightings of a gigantic worm within a glass-walled enclosure. Is it real or CGI? It's hard to be sure, but it might be real.

The Japanese Kappa

5.4 JAPAN'S KAPPA: RIVER MONSTERS AND THEIR TALES

Tales of the Kappa have lingered for centuries in Japan's lush, verdant landscapes, where rivers weave through mountains and fields. Deeply embedded in Japanese folklore, these water-dwelling creatures are depicted as small, human-like beings with webbed hands and feet, often with a turtle-like shell on their backs. The most distinctive feature of a Kappa is the dish-like depression sitting on its head, called a *sara*, filled with water. This peculiar characteristic is not just for show; the water is believed to be the source of the Kappa's power. If the water spills, the Kappa becomes weakened and cannot return to its watery home. In folklore, a Kappa is both mischievous and dangerous, capable of drowning unsuspecting travelers or livestock. Yet, they can also be tricked or befriended if approached with caution.

The Kappa's tales serve as cautionary narratives, particularly for children. These stories warn of the perils of venturing too close to water, using the Kappa to symbolize the hidden dangers lurking beneath calm surfaces. In this way, the Kappa becomes a guardian of water safety, instilling a healthy respect for nature's unpredictability. Beyond childhood warnings, the Kappa also plays a symbolic role in agricultural communities. The creature is said to aid farmers by irrigating fields, provided they are treated with respect and offered gifts, often cucumbers, the Kappa's favorite treat. This relationship highlights a deeper connection between humans and the natural world, emphasizing the importance of harmony and mutual respect.

Interestingly, the Kappa's behavior also reflects societal values, particularly the virtue of politeness. A Kappa is obsessed with manners and will bow in return if greeted with a bow. This gesture causes the water in their sara to spill, rendering them powerless. The deeper and more polite the bow, the more likely their water will spill and weaken them. This tale underscores the cultural importance of politeness and respect in Japanese society, serving as a moral lesson disguised within a folk narrative. Through these stories, the Kappa embodies the nuanced balance between danger and civility, a reminder of the unpredictable nature of the world and the social norms that help navigate it.

Modern interpretations of the Kappa often draw from contemporary scientific perspectives, offering explanations that bridge myth and reality. Some suggest that sightings of Kappa could stem from encounters with the Japanese giant salamander, an amphibious creature native to the region. With their semi-aquatic lifestyle and distinctive appearance, these salamanders might easily be mistaken for something more otherworldly, especially in dim light or murky waters. Cultural interpretations also play a role in maintaining the Kappa's presence in folklore. The stories adapt and evolve, reflecting the changing values and beliefs of Japanese society while retaining their core elements.

In popular culture, the Kappa has found new life in various media, from anime and manga to films and literature. These adaptations often portray the Kappa as whimsical characters, blending their mischievous nature with humor and charm. In anime, Kappa appears as both allies and antagonists; their stories are woven into narratives that explore broader themes of friendship and adventure. The influence of Kappa legends on Japanese art and literature is profound, with their image used to bring a sense of nostalgia and cultural heritage. This continued presence in modern story-telling ensures that the Kappa remains a vibrant part of Japan's cultural tapestry, bridging the gap between ancient lore and contemporary imagination.

As we conclude this exploration of Asian cryptids, we've seen how these creatures, from the Yeti to the Kappa, capture the imagination and reflect cultural values. Their stories serve as windows into the societies that created them, offering insight into human nature and our relationship with the unknown. In the next chapter, we will focus on the diverse cryptids of Africa and the Middle East, where the legends continue.

SIX
AFRICAN AND MIDDLE EASTERN ENIGMAS

The Mokele-Mbembe

IN THE HEART OF AFRICA, where the Congo River carves its way through dense jungles and uncharted territories, is the land of Mokele-Mbembe. This creature defies conventional understanding and dares us to reconsider what we think we know about the world. Mokele-Mbembe, whose name means "one who stops the flow of rivers" in Lingala, is said to inhabit the remote swamps and river systems of the Congo Basin. Local legends describe it as a massive, dinosaur-like being with a long neck and tail, reminiscent of the sauropods that roamed the Earth millions of years ago. This creature is more than a myth; it is woven into the region's cultural fabric.

The Mokele-Mbembe

6.1 THE MOKELE-MBEMBE: A LIVING DINOSAUR

Accounts of Mokele-Mbembe have been passed down through generations, painting a picture of a creature that is both revered and feared. In Congolese culture, Mokele-Mbembe is portrayed as a guardian of its domain, a protector of the waterways that sustain life. Yet, it is also seen as a threat, a territorial beast that will defend its home against intruders. This duality reflects the complex relationship that the people of the Congo have with their environment, which is both nurturing and hazardous. Eyewitness testimonies, particularly from the Pygmy tribes who inhabit the region, add depth to the legend. They speak of encounters with a creature that commands respect due to its size. This being remains elusive despite many attempts to document its existence.

In the 1980s, the legend of Mokele-Mbembe captured the attention of biologist Roy Mackal, who led expeditions into the heart of the Congo Basin in search of evidence. These expeditions were marked by anticipation and frustration, as the dense jungle and challenging terrain made the search dangerous and difficult. Mackal's team, armed with scientific equipment and determined to uncover the truth, gathered stories from locals and searched for physical evidence, such as tracks or nests. Although they returned with compelling anecdotes, they found no definitive proof.

The contribution of cryptozoologists in this ongoing quest is essential, as they continue to investigate whether Mokele-Mbembe could be a surviving remnant of Earth's prehistoric past. Some cryptozoologists speculate that the creature could be a living sauropod, a relic from an era when dinosaurs ruled the land. This theory, while tantalizing, faces significant challenges. The feasibility of such a large animal surviving in the modern era without leaving substantial physical evidence, such as bones or clear photographs, seems unlikely. Skeptics argue that the dense and biodiverse Congo Basin, although largely unexplored, should have revealed more concrete evidence of a creature as large as a sauropod. The lack of such evidence makes many question whether Mokele-Mbembe is a reality or a myth born from the region's rich storytelling tradition.

The cultural impact of Mokele-Mbembe extends beyond the realm of legend, influencing national identity and scientific curiosity. In the Congo, the creature symbolizes the mysterious and untamed forces that shape the land, reflecting the untapped potential of the natural world. Mokele-Mbembe has also become a focal point for ecotourism, drawing adventurers and researchers eager to explore the region's secrets. This interest has spurred conservation efforts to preserve the delicate ecosystems that may harbor such enigmatic life. The idea of Mokele-Mbembe continues to inspire modern research, helping us learn more about the Congo Basin's complex ecosystem.

The Marozi

6.2 THE MAROZI: AFRICA'S SPOTTED LION

In the heart of Kenya's Aberdare Mountains, a creature of legend prowls the dense forests and open plains. Known as the Marozi, this enigmatic feline has captivated locals and visitors with its unique characteristics. Unlike the majestic lions that roam the savannas, the Marozi is said to possess a coat with spots like a leopard's. This striking feature sets it apart, sparking intrigue and debate among those who seek to understand its origins. Historical accounts from the early 20th-century speak of encounters with this elusive animal, painting a picture of a creature that defies conventional classification. Sightings often describe the Marozi as a lion in size and build, yet with the distinctive markings of a leopard, creating a hybrid image that challenges our understanding of African wildlife.

The legend of the Marozi gained traction in the 1930s when British colonists and game wardens reported sightings of this unusual creature. Often detailed and compelling, these reports added credibility to the tales circulating among local communities. Photographic evidence, though scarce, has been analyzed by zoologists seeking to unravel the mystery. Some images, albeit grainy, appear to show the Marozi in its natural habitat, its coat a patchwork of spots and tawny fur. While not definitive, these photographs provide a tantalizing glimpse into the possibility of the Marozi's existence. They also fuel the ongoing debate among scientists and enthusiasts, each eager to uncover the truth behind this cryptid's legend.

There are many theories regarding the Marozi's origins, which reflect the natural world's complexity. Some suggest that the Marozi may result from a genetic mutation where a lion retains juvenile spots into adulthood. This theory posits that environmental pressures in the Aberdare Mountains might favor such traits, allowing them to persist in a small population. Others speculate that the Marozi could be a product of hybridization between lions and leopards. However, this explanation faces challenges, as lions and leopards rarely interbreed in the wild due to differing behaviors and habitats. The frequency of Marozi sightings further complicates this theory, as one would expect fewer instances if hybridization were the sole cause. Environmental adaptation offers another possibility, suggesting that the Marozi's distinctive coat provides camouflage in the dappled light of the forest, enhancing its survival in this unique ecosystem.

Beyond its biological intrigue, the Marozi holds significant cultural value in Kenyan folklore and identity. It symbolizes the mysteries of the natural world, embodying the unknown that lies beyond the reach of modern science. Stories of the Marozi, passed down through generations, enrich the region's cultural history, reflecting the deep connection between the people and the land. These narratives, while rooted in legend, also inspire contemporary conservation efforts. The potential existence of the Marozi highlights the importance of preserving Kenya's diverse ecosystems, where undiscovered species may still roam. Conservation strategies increasingly recognize the role of local folklore in fostering a sense of stewardship, using the allure of cryptids like the Marozi to engage communities in protecting their natural heritage, thereby also protecting known animals and their habitat.

The Marozi's story continues to captivate those who hear it, drawing researchers and storytellers into its world. Whether a product of myth, genetic anomaly, or undiscovered species, the Marozi invites us to look closer at the world around us. It challenges our assumptions and encourages a deeper appreciation for the complexities of nature. As we consider the Marozi's place in the wild, we are reminded of the vast potential for discovery that still exists in the uncharted areas of our planet. Through its legend, the Marozi invites us to explore, question, and preserve the fragile balance of life everywhere.

The Djinn

6.3 DJINN AND CRYPTIDS: MYTHS OF THE MIDDLE EAST

In the ancient cities of the Middle East, stories about Djinn play an important role in the culture. These tales blend imagination with reality, creating a rich history. Djinn are mysterious beings found in Arabian folklore for centuries, captivating both storytellers and listeners with their power. They can shapeshift and take on human or animal forms. Unlike simple spirits, Djinn are complex and real. They are similar to angels in that they are powerful but different because they have freedom and make moral choices. The Qur'an describes them as creatures made from smokeless fire, existing alongside humans but hidden from view. Djinn can choose to be good or evil, reflecting the moral complexities of human nature.

Djinn represent more than just myths. They symbolize the unseen forces of nature and the universe that we cannot fully understand. In many stories passed down through generations, Djinn serve as cautionary figures, showing the consequences of uncontrolled desires or the dangers of challenging the unknown. These tales provide moral lessons against greed, pride, and curiosity that crosses boundaries. Djinn remind us of the limits of our knowledge and the vast forces that shape our world. Through these stories, they mirror the fears and hopes that influence societies.

Djinn have significantly impacted literature and media, appealing to audiences with their intrigue and depth. One well-known collection, "One Thousand and One Nights," features Djinn as key characters interacting with humans, offering gifts, challenges, or punishment. These imaginative stories have spread beyond the Middle East, shaping global storytelling. Djinn also appear in many films and TV shows, whether as friends or foes, highlighting their ongoing fascination and the universal themes they represent.

Modern views on Djinn continue to change, influenced by today's perspectives and cultural exchanges. New stories about encounters with Djinn arise from the Middle East, adding to the rich diversity of modern folklore. These tales keep the legend alive and reveal how people perceive Djinn today. In urban legends and popular culture, Djinn often straddle the line between reality and imagination, linking ancient beliefs with modern skepticism. They serve as real beings and symbols for the unknown, capturing the curiosity of those who want to understand life's mysteries.

When we examine these tales, we can see how much Djinn have influenced the cultural and spiritual landscape of the Middle East. Their stories teach us and push us to think about existence and the unseen forces that shape our lives. Through Djinn, we gain a greater appreciation for the rich folklore of different cultures.

Contemporary images of Djinn on social media seem to focus on their demonic tendencies, with videos tending toward the dark and paranormal. If you choose to watch anything that might be dark or demonic, always protect yourself in a manner consistent with your higher power or religious beliefs. I personally avoid anything dark or demonic, but if I must look at something like the mentioned videos, I surround myself with

Angels and prayer. I have included a photo of the powerful protector Archangel Michael to help you if you wish.

Archangel Michael, helper and protector

The Grootslang

6.4 THE GROOTSLANG: A TALE FROM SOUTH AFRICA

In the vast, rugged terrain of South Africa's Richtersveld region, legends speak of a creature that defies description and logic—a mythical beast known as the Grootslang. This creature is said to be a massive serpent with fearsome tusks, blending the features of a snake and an elephant. Its tale is deeply rooted in South African folklore, particularly among the Venda and Afrikaner cultures, where it is believed to dwell in a cavern known as the "Wonder Hole" or "Bottomless Pit." This cave, rumored to be filled with diamonds, adds an element of intrigue and allure to the Grootslang's myth, intertwining wealth and danger in a narrative that has captivated imaginations for generations.

The Grootslang is more than a creature of myth; it is an enduring symbol of the untamed and ancient landscape it inhabits. According to legend, its origins date back to the dawn of time, when the gods created the first creatures. The Grootslang was so powerful and fearsome that the gods, realizing their mistake, split it into two separate animals: the elephant and the snake. However, one Grootslang escaped this fate, finding refuge in the depths of the earth, where it has remained ever since. This narrative highlights the creature's formidable nature and reflects the themes of balance and duality prevalent in many cultural stories.

Reports of Grootslang sightings have sparked intrigue and fear, particularly in the Richtersveld region, where the creature is said to make its home. The disappearance of Englishman Peter Grayson in 1917, who ventured into these caves in search of treasure, adds a layer of mystery and caution to the legend. His fate remains unknown, fueling speculation that the Grootslang was responsible. South African prospector Lt. Fred Cornell's encounters in 1910 and 1920 further contribute to the tale. Cornell claimed to have seen the creature, describing its massive size and terrifying presence. He even resorted to using dynamite to dislodge it, which speaks to the desperation and fear it inspired. Eyewitness accounts from diamond miners, who report sightings of enormous tracks and eerie sounds echoing from the caverns, lend credence to the legend, keeping it alive in the hearts and minds of those who work and live there.

From a scientific perspective, the existence of the Grootslang is met with skepticism. Some theories suggest that the creature could be a misinterpretation of known animals, such as large snakes, monitor lizards, or crocodiles that inhabit the region. These species, while impressive in their own right, lack the mythical characteristics attributed to the Grootslang, leading scientists to question the plausibility of such a creature. Skeptics point to the lack of concrete evidence—no remains, clear photographs, or biological traces have been found to support the Grootslang's existence. Yet, the rich geological features of the Richtersveld, with its intricate cave systems and rugged landscape, provide ample fodder for the imagination, allowing the legend to persist.

The cultural impact of the Grootslang extends beyond folklore, influencing both South African storytelling and tourism. The creature stands as a symbol of the wild and untamed beauty of the region, embodying the allure that draws adventurers and tourists alike. The legend of the Grootslang has become a part of the fabric of South African identity, reflecting the country's rich heritage and the interplay between myth and reality. Adventure tourism in the area capitalizes on this allure, offering guided tours and expeditions into the caves where the Grootslang is said to dwell. While focused on exploration and discovery, these ventures also perpetuate the legend, ensuring that the Grootslang remains an integral part of South African culture and storytelling.

As we close this chapter, the Grootslang invites us to reflect on the power of myth that continues to captivate us. This chapter has explored the rich tapestry of African and Middle Eastern cryptids, each unique and compelling in its own right. Whether based on reality or from imagination, these legends remind us of the diverse and complex narratives shaping our understanding of the world. In the next chapter, we will investigate the cryptids of Oceania, where new tales await.

Make a Difference with Your Review

Unlock the Power of Discovery

"The world is full of unexplained mysteries, waiting for those brave enough to search for the truth." – Unknown

Curiosity drives discovery, and the search for the unknown is what makes life exciting. Now, you have a chance to help others on their journey into the world of cryptids!

Would you help someone just like you—eager to learn about the creatures of legend but unsure where to start?

My mission in *Cryptids of the World, Where Legends Meet Reality* is to explore these fascinating beings in a way that sparks imagination, curiosity, and adventure. But to reach more people, I need your help.

Most readers choose books based on reviews. That's why your review is so important. A few sentences from you could help someone take the first step into the world of cryptids.

It costs nothing, takes less than a minute, but could inspire someone's next great adventure. Your review could help...

...one more reader dive into the mystery.

...one more explorer set out on their own search.

...one more skeptic open their mind to possibilities.

...one more believer find the stories they crave.

...one more dream take flight.

If you love uncovering mysteries and helping others, you're my kind of person. Thank you for being part of this journey!

Karen E. Mueller, DVM

SEVEN
CRYPTIDS OF OCEANIA

The Bunyip

IN AUSTRALIA, the Bunyip is a legendary folklore creature often seen as a fearsome water-dweller inhabiting swamps, billabongs, creeks, and lagoons. Descriptions of the Bunyip vary, with some saying it looks like an amphibious monster with an elongated neck and a cross between an ox and a hippopotamus. Others depict it as having a human-like figure. Its booming or roaring cries resonate across the water, adding to its mysterious and fearful reputation.

The Bunyip

7.1 THE BUNYIP: ABORIGINAL WATER PROTECTOR

The Bunyip is deeply rooted in Aboriginal culture, where it is seen as both a physical being and a spiritual guardian of the waterways. Aboriginal stories often portray the Bunyip as a protector of the land, emphasizing respect for nature and balance in the environment. In the Dreaming, a foundational piece of Aboriginal belief, the Bunyip takes a significant place, highlighting the interconnectedness of the physical and spiritual realms. It serves as a warning about the dangers near water, teaching lessons about caution and interconnectedness with nature.

Early European explorers found the Bunyip legend terrifying, as the 1890 illustration by Joseph Macfarlane demonstrates. In it, we see a fierce Bunyip shoulder-deep in swampy water with a man entirely gripped in its gigantic toothy jaws, presumably to be killed and / or eaten.

. . .

Some scientific theories suggest that the Bunyip legend could be based on misidentified native animals, like the platypus--an equally weird animal with its duck-like bill, webbed feet, and beaver-like tail. Similarly, the Bunyip's diverse descriptions may stem from rare sightings of seals that have ventured unusually far upstream. The strange sounds attributed to the Bunyip could also be from the bittern, a marsh bird known for its eerie cries.

Today, the Bunyip symbolizes Australian culture and is featured in literature, art, and children's stories that mix mystery and fun. Its legend inspires conservation efforts focused on protecting Australia's unique ecosystems, helping bridge the gap between ancient myths and modern conservation.

The Moehau

7.2 NEW ZEALAND'S MOEHAU: THE ISLAND SASQUATCH

In the dense, verdant forests of New Zealand's Coromandel Range, tales of a mysterious creature have persisted for generations. Known as the Moehau, this large, ape-like being has captured the imaginations of the indigenous Māori and European settlers. Descriptions of the Moehau often depict it as towering over the average human, with a hulking frame covered in shaggy hair. Its presence is marked by an eerie silence, broken only by the occasional rustle of leaves or distant call echoing through the forest. For the Māori, the Moehau is more than a cryptid; it is a figure deeply rooted in their cultural mythology. Stories of giant, human-like beings known as Maero populate Māori folklore, and the Moehau is often regarded as a modern iteration of these ancient legends. The narrative of the Moehau is interwoven with themes of respect for nature and the mysteries it holds, serving as a reminder of the untamed wilderness that surrounds us.

. . .

Sightings of the Moehau have been reported throughout the 20th century, with accounts coming from trampers, hunters, and residents who have ventured into the remote areas of the Coromandel. These encounters often describe a fleeting glimpse of a creature that seems to vanish into the dense undergrowth, leaving only footprints and the occasional hair sample as evidence. Despite the skepticism that often greets such sightings, they have spurred several expeditions by cryptozoologists eager to uncover the truth. One notable effort is the work of Marc Coppell, whose documentary "The X-rated Files: Followed from Skinwalker" delves into the existence of the Moehau. Coppell's investigations and those of other researchers have kept the legend alive, drawing attention to this elusive creature and the possibility of its existence. These trips spark interest in exploring the unknown, encouraging both scientific research and creative thinking.

From a scientific perspective, the Moehau's existence is met with intrigue and skepticism. Some theories suggest that sightings of the Moehau may be attributed to misidentified native species, such as the large and elusive feral pigs or even the endangered kaka, a native parrot with a surprisingly robust presence in the forest canopy. These animals might easily be mistaken for something else when glimpsed in low light or from a distance. Skeptics argue that the dense, isolated environment of New Zealand makes the existence of undiscovered large mammals unlikely. The country's unique ecosystem, which has evolved in isolation over millions of years, lacks the large predators and herbivores found in other parts of the world. This ecological context challenges the plausibility of a creature like the Moehau remaining hidden in modern times. However, the persistence of the Moehau in local lore and reported sightings suggests that the legend serves as more than mere misidentification; it is a symbol of the enduring mysteries of the natural world.

Culturally, the Moehau is significant in both Māori storytelling and New Zealand's broader heritage. For the Māori, the Moehau is a testament to their rich oral tradition, preserving the stories of their ancestors and the landscapes they inhabit. These narratives reinforce a connection to the land, celebrating its beauty and enigma. In contemporary New Zealand, the Moehau contributes to the nation's cultural identity as a point of intrigue and pride. The creature's legend has inspired elements of New Zealand tourism, drawing visitors eager to explore the lush forests and rugged terrain that might conceal such a cryptid. Media representations have further cemented the Moehau's place in the public consciousness, with documentaries and articles exploring the legend and its implications. This cultural impact underscores the power of myth and storytelling in shaping our understanding of the world, inviting us to question, explore, and, ultimately, to wonder.

Hawaiian Night Marchers

7.3 HAWAIIAN NIGHT MARCHERS: SPIRITS OR CRYPTIDS?

In the lush landscapes of Hawaii, where the ocean meets the mountains, the legend of the Night Marchers is deeply rooted in local folklore. These spectral apparitions are said to be the spirits of ancient Hawaiian warriors marching in solemn procession across the islands. The distant sound of beating drums signals their presence, the haunting call of a conch shell, and the eerie glow of torchlight cutting through the night. These processions are not mere ghostly wanderings; they serve as a powerful reminder of the past, a manifestation of these warriors' sacred duty to protect their chiefs and sacred sites. The Night Marchers are believed to traverse paths that connect significant historical locations, reinforcing their role as guardians of the land. This connection to sacred sites underscores their spiritual significance, embodying the reverence with which these places are held in Hawaiian culture.

The symbolism of the Night Marchers extends beyond the mere appearance of ghostly warriors. They embody the deep respect for ancestors and the spiritual ties that bind the present to the past. In Hawaiian belief, the Night Marchers are revered as figures of ancestral power, reminding the living of the importance of honoring those who have come before. If you see one, you will die, but you will be protected if you have an ancestor within the night marchers. Their processions serve as a lesson in respect, teaching that sacred lands and traditions must be preserved and honored. This reverence for the past is woven into the societal values of Hawaii, where the land is seen as a living thing, imbued with the mana, or spiritual energy, of those who have walked it before. In this context, the Night Marchers are both protectors and reminders of the sacred, urging us all to walk on this earth with respect.

The tales of the Night Marchers have become an integral part of Hawaiian identity, influencing cultural perception and tourism. Stories of these ghostly processions captivate locals and visitors alike, drawing them into the rich history of Hawaiian myth. In literature and media, the Night Marchers are portrayed with a blend of awe and fear, reflecting the complex emotions they evoke. Their legend is a focal point in cultural education, offering a lens through which the values and beliefs of Hawaiian society can be understood. For tourists, the allure of the Night Marchers adds a mystical dimension to the islands, inviting them to explore Hawaii's physical beauty and spiritual depth. This legend adds to the cultural experience and tells stories of the islands that connect with the past.

Eyewitness accounts of the Night Marchers add an element of intrigue and authenticity to their legend. Residents and visitors have reported encounters that defy explanation, with tales of spectral figures and the unmistakable sound of marching feet echoing through the night. Hawaiian oral traditions, with their emphasis on the spoken word and communal sharing of history, play a crucial role in maintaining the vibrancy of these tales. This living tradition connects us to the past. The stories of the Night Marchers change over time but still hold deep meaning. When you listen to these stories, you join a long history that links history and myth.

See the YouTube video 89, Hauka'i Po (Night Marchers) on the No'eau Woo-O'Brien channel for a senior Hawaiian elder relating her story of an encounter with the Night Marchers as a young girl.

Reflection Section: Personal Connection to Folklore

Consider how folklore and legends have shaped your understanding of place and identity. Have you encountered stories or myths that resonate with your own experiences or beliefs? Reflect on how these narratives influence your connection to the land and culture around you.

The Yara-ma-yha-who

7.4 THE YARA-MA-YHA-WHO: MYTHS OF THE OUTBACK

In the sunny Australian Outback, where the land is filled with red soil and gum trees, the story of the Yara-ma-yha-who comes to life. This diminutive creature, a staple of Aboriginal folklore, is unlike any other mythological tale. It is described as a small, red, frog-like being with a voracious thirst for blood. Its huge head and gaping mouth, devoid of teeth, give it an unsettling appearance. The creature is said to reside in fig trees, waiting with eerie patience for an unwary traveler to rest below. This parasitic ambush predator drops down on its prey, using the suckers on its hands and feet to drain their blood before swallowing them whole. After a brief nap, it regurgitates its prey, now changed in some creepy, subtle way. This terrifying and vicious cycle can transform the victim into another Yara-ma-yha-who, perpetuating the legend and fueling the fear of the unknown that permeates the land.

The Yara-ma-yha-who holds a significant place in the rich world of Aboriginal mythology, where it serves as both a creature of the physical realm and a symbol of the outback's untamed essence. This creature embodies the harshness and mystery of the Australian interior, where survival often depends on understanding the delicate balance between humans and nature. Its presence in myth underscores a deep respect for the hidden dangers of the land. For the Aboriginal peoples, the Yara-ma-yha-who is more than a tale to frighten children; it reminds them of the interconnectedness of all living things and the spirits that inhabit the earth. This myth also serves as a cautionary tale, warning the young about the perils of wandering alone, especially in the vast, open spaces of the outback. Through stories shared around campfires and in the oral traditions passed down through generations, the Yara-ma-yha-who teaches lessons of vigilance and respect, encapsulating the societal values and wisdom of the Aboriginal cultures.

Modern interpretations of the Yara-ma-yha-who have taken on new dimensions as contemporary audiences seek to understand its significance beyond the realm of folklore. Some view the creature as a metaphor for environmental challenges, representing the impact of human actions on the natural world. In this light, the Yara-ma-yha-who symbolizes nature's resilience and the unintended consequences of disrupting ecological balance. Its role in Australian horror and fantasy genres further amplifies this narrative, where the creature's eerie nature and unique abilities capture the imagination of storytellers and audiences alike. The Yara-ma-yha-who, with its blend of fear and fascination, fits seamlessly into stories that explore the boundaries between reality and myth, providing a rich source of inspiration for writers and filmmakers who seek to delve into the darker corners of the human psyche.

The cultural impact of the Yara-ma-yha-who extends beyond entertainment, influencing how Australians perceive their heritage and identity. As a key figure in Aboriginal storytelling, the creature plays a valuable role in preserving cultural narratives and educating new generations about the traditions of their ancestors. The Yara-ma-yha-who features prominently in the works of Aboriginal authors, such as David Unaipon, who have shared these stories with broader audiences. Unaipon, known for his contributions to literature and advocacy for Indigenous rights, has helped bring the Yara-ma-yha-who to the forefront of cultural consciousness, ensuring its place in the collective memory of Australia. Educational programs that focus on Aboriginal myths often include the Yara-ma-yha-who, using its story to teach children about the importance of cultural preservation and the lessons embedded within these ancient tales.

As this chapter ends, we look at the broader effects of these myths on the cultures they belong to. The legends of Oceania, like the Yara-ma-yha-who, highlight important themes of respect, survival, and connection. However, many mysteries still await beyond the horizon.

EIGHT
LATIN AMERICAN LEGENDS

The Chupacabra

IN PUERTO RICO, storytelling is a common way to spend an evening. One popular tale is the legend of the Chupacabra, a fearful and notorious creature said to attack livestock. This story began in the mid-1990s when reports of goats found drained of their blood shocked a small town. Described as a reptilian creature with spikes along its back, the Chupacabra quickly gained fame across Latin America and beyond, with its chilling story.

The Chupacabra

8.1 THE CHUPACABRA: LATIN AMERICAN PREDATOR

Sightings of the Chupacabra spread to rural areas in Latin America and the southern United States, with witnesses describing it as having glowing eyes and an insatiable thirst for blood. Although the details varied in each account, they conveyed a shared fear and dread. The media played a key role in making the Chupacabra a household name through sensational headlines and stories, often blending fact with fiction.

On the other hand, many scientists have suggested that the Chupacabra might be attributed to normal animals like coyotes suffering from severe mange. This condition, caused by parasitic mites, can make them look odd, from partially bald with flaky skin to completely hairless. This could lead witnesses to think they saw something supernatural. In effect, they may simply have witnessed a natural animal. While this explanation seems logical, many still cling to the myth of the Chupacabra. Some scientists and skeptics question the creature's existence due to the lack of physical evidence and necropsy results confirming blood draining as a mark of the Chupacabra.

The Chupacabra has significantly influenced culture and has become part of the folklore of Latin America. It's a perfect example of how supernatural stories blend with everyday life. Its notoriety has led to its appearance in various media, movies, and literature. This story is also a good example of how urban legends can develop and stay powerful within a culture. It highlights the lasting power of storytelling in shaping our views of the world.

Few contemporary eyewitness reports exist, and no video or still camera footage of any reptilian-like creature that might be ascribed to Chupacabra is available on social media. However, on TikTok, one can find videos of a canid-like creature that people are calling Chupacabra. One such creature, which was live-trapped, appeared to be an unknown canid with front feet that gripped the cage much like a raccoon's front paws would. It will be interesting to discover if this canid is a previously unidentified species.

El Silbón

8.2 EL SILBÓN: THE WHISTLING GHOST OF VENEZUELA

In the plains of Venezuela, where the horizon stretches under a canopy of stars, tales of El Silbón resonate through the night with a chilling echo. This spectral figure, known as The Whistler, is deeply rooted in the folklore of Los Llanos, an expansive region of grasslands and savannas. The origins of this legend are not fully understood but seem to trace back to a strange tale of familial betrayal and vengeance, possibly stemming from a gruesome murder around 1850. The story tells of a young boy who, in a fit of rage, murdered his father for failing to bring him deer meat. When he discovered that the meat served to him was the organs of his father, the boy's mother cursed him, and his grandfather punished him severely, setting the stage for his transformation into El Silbón.

El Silbón is characterized by his eerie whistle, a sound that defies logic and instills dread. The closer his whistle seems, the farther away he is; when it fades into the distance, he is perilously close. This whistling illusion adds to his ominous presence, leaving those who hear it in a state of anxious foreboding. His spectral figure is often described as gaunt and towering, cloaked in shadows, while his wide-brimmed hat casts a permanent shroud over his face. He is said to target drunks, perhaps a nod to his grandfather's punishment, which involved whipping his grandson and then washing his wounds with alcohol and chilis. He is also known to haunt womanizers, visiting his wrath upon those who stray from loyalty. With their instinctual aversion to the supernatural, dogs provide the only effective deterrent against El Silbón. Their furious barking drives him away since he loathes these potentially rabid creatures for having attacked him in the past.

El Silbón is a potent symbol in Venezuelan culture, embodying themes of guilt, remorse, and retribution. As a cautionary tale, he warns of the consequences of disrespecting one's family and the moral decay that follows betrayal. His story is a reminder of the societal values that prioritize familial bonds and the inherent dangers of failing to uphold them. El Silbón symbolizes the burden of guilt and the unavoidable consequences of one's past sins. His eternal wandering through the plains represents unresolved remorse, a ghostly embodiment of the emotional burdens that trouble the living.

El Silbón continues to shape the cultural identity and captivate the public imagination in modern Venezuela. His legend has been immortalized in literature and media, from haunting tales in local anthologies to eerie depictions in television series. These portrayals keep the myth alive, blending traditional storytelling with contemporary narratives. Local festivals and celebrations often feature El Silbón as a central figure, with reenactments and performances that bring the legend to life. Such events not only entertain but also reinforce cultural ties and collective memory, ensuring that the story of El Silbón endures through the generations.

The power of oral tradition plays an important role in perpetuating the legend of El Silbón. These stories are passed down through families, shared around campfires and during community gatherings, preserving the narrative's authenticity and emotional impact. Storytelling becomes a communal experience, a way to connect with the past and affirm cultural identity. Through these narratives, El Silbón remains a living legend, a testament to the enduring power of folklore in shaping the human experience.

In the rural areas of Venezuela and Colombia, eyewitness accounts abound, with people recounting chilling encounters with the whistling ghost. Interviews with locals reveal a deep-seated belief in El Silbón's existence, with many expressing a genuine fear of his presence. However, internet searches did not reveal any significant results for positive sightings of El Silbón.

The Mapinguari

8.3 THE MAPINGUARI: AMAZONIAN GIANT

The Amazon rainforest is a dense and vibrant place full of life, mystery, and danger. Among its many stories is the legend of the Mapinguari, a creature that people both fear and respect. Some say it looks like a giant sloth; some say it's more like a Sasquatch, and has a terrifying feature—a mouth in the middle of its stomach. The Mapinguari is a powerful and important figure in Amazonian folklore. Indigenous tribes view it as a guardian of the forest, reminding people to live in harmony with the environment to avoid angering the creature and inciting its wrath.

Many indigenous communities claim to have seen the Mapinguari. They describe it as a large, hairy, foul-smelling creature that vanishes into the forest upon sight. These accounts have led cryptozoologists to explore the Amazon seeking proof of its existence. David Oren led one notable expedition in 1993, but it didn't find any conclusive evidence. Still, the stories continue to attract researchers and adventurers alike.

• • •

Some scientists think the Mapinguari might be a surviving giant ground sloth, an animal that lived in the Americas during the last Ice Age. These sloths were much larger than those seen today and are believed to have gone extinct around 10,000 years ago. However, a 2023 study on giant sloth bones found in the Amazon suggests that humans might have coexisted with these creatures, which could have inspired the Mapinguari legend. The modified bones, turned into jewelry, show that these sloths held cultural significance that may connect myth to reality. Skeptics argue that finding such a large animal is unlikely even with modern exploration methods like drones and satellite imagery. Yet, interest in the unknown continues, along with the possibility of such a creature living in the Amazon and the excitement of its possible discovery.

The legend of the Mapinguari greatly influences local culture. In stories, it acts as both a protector and a warning. This dual role shows a strong respect for nature, which is essential to the local cultural heritage. The Mapinguari also helps promote ecotourism, which encourages visitors to explore the beauty of the Amazon and supports conservation efforts to protect its rich biodiversity. Some people see similarities between the Mapinguari and North America's Sasquatch. Both are described as large, hairy creatures with a putrid smell. Reports of the Mapinguari also mention large footprints and long, frightening-looking claws on its front feet. However, the footprints of the Mapinguari are described as round rather than human-like, similar to those of ancient sloths. These similarities between myths of Amazonian Mapinguari and North American Sasquatch stories suggest a universal human interest in mysterious creatures, or perhaps the extensive range of the creatures in the Sasquatch-type family.

You can find footage on YouTube of Animal Planet's expedition into the Amazon in search of the Mapinguari. Although they don't have an actual sighting, they hear wood knocks, which are well-known signs of Sasquatch. Beyond this, online searches for Mapinguari sightings were unproductive.

La Llorona

8.4 LA LLORONA: A WEEPING WARNING

Amidst Latin America's quiet, moonlit nights, the wail of La Llorona, the Weeping Woman, drifts through the air, causing a chill down the spine of those who hear it. A spectral figure, her sorrowful lament resonates deeply within the region's cultural fabric. Her story is one of tragedy and remorse, rooted in the rich history of Latin American folklore. La Llorona is often described as a ghostly woman in white, forever mourning the loss of her children, whom she drowned in a fit of madness. Her tale serves as a poignant reminder of the themes of grief and redemption, as she wanders the earth in eternal penance, searching for her lost children. This narrative, passed down through generations, has become a cornerstone of Latin American storytelling, intertwining historical context with cultural values.

The character of La Llorona is steeped in symbolism, portraying universal themes that transcend time and place. She embodies the essence of maternal responsibility, a cautionary tale warning against the perils of neglect and despair. Her story reflects societal beliefs about the sanctity of motherhood and the consequences of failing to uphold these ideals. Beyond this, La Llorona represents universal sorrow, her cries echoing the collective grief that resonates with anyone who has experienced loss. Her presence in folklore provides a channel for expressing difficult emotions, offering a space for reflection and understanding. Through her story, people, families, and communities explore complex human emotions and struggle to find peace amidst turmoil.

La Llorona continues to significantly influence contemporary Latin American culture, shaping identity and captivating the imagination. Her legend has been reinterpreted countless times, from haunting tales in literature to vivid films and other media depictions. These portrayals keep her story alive, inviting new interpretations and broader audiences. Local festivals and celebrations often feature La Llorona as a central figure, with performances and reenactments that bring her story to life. These events reinforce cultural ties and collective memory, ensuring that the story of La Llorona remains a vital part of the regional identity. Her tale resonates as a ghostly legend and reflects the human experience, bridging the past and present through shared stories.

The power of oral tradition plays a crucial role in perpetuating the legend of La Llorona. Across Latin America, the practice of storytelling keeps her story alive and vivid with emotional depth. Communities gather to share tales of encounters with the Weeping Woman, each adding layers to the richness of her story. These narratives often contain practical warnings, cautioning children against venturing too close to rivers, lakes, and drainage ditches. While rooted in myth, such tales carry real-world lessons, emphasizing the importance of safety and awareness. Eyewitness accounts from various regions further enhance the legend, with many describing sightings of a woman in white, her cries echoing through the night as she floats just above the ground towards them. These real or imagined encounters contribute to the enduring power of La Llorona's story, ensuring her place in the cultural consciousness.

Many people in Latin America sincerely believe in La Llorona. Eyewitness accounts of her can be found online, and some of them are compelling.

. . .

As we conclude this chapter, the legends of Latin America reveal the intricate dance between myth and reality, shaping cultural identities and reflecting societal values. These tales, deeply embedded in the region's folklore, invite us to explore the mysteries of the human experience and the lasting allure of the unknown.

NINE
HUMAN ACTIVITY ON CRYPTID HABITATS AND CONSERVATION

Sasquatch, or Bigfoot

IN THE SHADOW of human progress, where the relentless march of development meets the edge of the wild, the habitats of cryptids face unprecedented challenges. If you visit some Pacific Northwest national parks, you might stand in the heart of a vast, ancient forest, where the air is thick with the scent of pine and the sounds of life. Here, tales of Bigfoot have flourished for generations. Yet, the very forests that conceal such mysteries are under siege. Human encroachment through logging and urbanization carves into these ecosystems, disrupting the delicate balance of life. As trees fall for buildings and paper products, and concrete sprawls ever outward, the wilderness recedes, pushing its inhabitants—both known and unknown—into ever-smaller refuges. This encroachment fragments habitats into smaller pieces, creating isolated pockets where creatures must adapt or disappear.

In Skamania County, Washington, a unique legal measure reflects a cultural reverence for the unknown. The county prohibits harming Sasquatch, an actual legal acknowledgment of the connection between the land and its legendary inhabitants. Such cultural efforts highlight a recognition that preserving these habitats is crucial, not only for the potential existence of cryptids but also for the myriad of species that call these forests home. Urban sprawl, with its ever-expanding reach, forces wildlife to adapt to changing environments and new realities. As animals venture into suburban landscapes, sightings of unfamiliar creatures increase, sparking new myths and legends. The intersection of nature and human habitation blurs the lines between the possible and the improbable, feeding the human imagination and, ultimately, the stories we tell.

Turning our gaze to the waters of Loch Ness, we find another tale where human activity intersects with legend. Pollution, a byproduct of industrialization and agriculture, seeps into the loch, altering its ecosystem. As the water quality changes, so too might the behaviors and habitats of its inhabitants, potentially influencing sightings of the famed Loch Ness Monster. Rising temperatures compound these changes, affecting aquatic ecosystems, the snowpack, and glaciers of the mountains like the Himalayas. The Yeti, a creature rooted in the high-altitude myths of the region, may find its patterns of life altered as the climate shifts. As glaciers retreat and temperatures climb, the habitats supporting such legends evolve, challenging the real and imagined creatures that navigate these landscapes.

Reflection Section: Consider Your Impact on Local Ecosystems

Reflect on your community and its natural surroundings. How does human activity shape these environments? Consider your role in conservation efforts and how you might support local ecosystems. Could you bike to work to avoid using fossil fuels? Could you volunteer to help maintain your local green space? In our community, we firmly commit to green energy, and many people add solar panels to their homes to support it. We also have groups that restore creeks for salmon and accept volunteer workers. You could do anything from using less plastic to cleaning up your local beach. Anything you do to impact the environment around you, even in your own home, even in a tiny way, makes a difference.

These reflections deepen our understanding of cryptid habitats and prompt us to consider the broader implications of our actions. The stories of cryptids, intertwined with environmental change, serve as reminders of the interconnectedness of all life. As we navigate the complexities of conservation in an ever-changing world, the legends of mythical beings continue to inspire curiosity and stewardship, urging us to protect the habitats around us.

"Save the Yeti" campaign

9.1 CONSERVATION EFFORTS INSPIRED BY CRYPTID MYTHS

Stories of legendary creatures captivate our imaginations and drive us to protect the natural world. These myths, rich in cultural heritage and mystery, are increasingly leveraged as powerful tools for conservation. In the Himalayas, for instance, the legend of the Yeti has transcended folklore to inspire real-world action. The "Save the Yeti" campaign has become a rallying cry, focusing efforts on preserving the fragile ecosystems of the Himalayas. By invoking the Yeti, this campaign draws attention to the region's broader environmental challenges, from deforestation to climate change. It engages both locals and the international community, reminding us of the intrinsic value of these landscapes and the need to safeguard them for future generations.

Similarly, the Amazon rainforest, sometimes called the "lungs of the Earth," finds its champion in the Mapinguari—the enormous, mythical creature said to inhabit its depths. Conservation projects in the Amazon have embraced the Mapinguari legend as a symbol of the forest's untamed beauty and mystery. These initiatives aim to protect the rainforest from the relentless pressures of logging and agriculture. By framing conservation within the context of the Mapinguari, these efforts tap into local folklore to emphasize the importance of preserving the unique biodiversity of the Amazon. The legend serves as a reminder of the interconnectedness of all living things, urging us to protect the intricate web of life below the canopy of the Amazon trees.

Community involvement and Indigenous leadership are at the heart of many conservation efforts inspired by cryptid myths. Across the globe, Indigenous communities have long revered the natural world as sacred, weaving their stories and beliefs into their conservation practices. These communities lead the charge in protecting habitats linked to their folklore, recognizing the symbiotic relationship between the health of their culture and that of their surroundings. Indigenous-led conservation initiatives draw on cryptid stories to inspire community ownership and action, fostering a sense of responsibility for preserving the land and its creatures. These efforts often result in innovative conservation strategies prioritizing sustainability and respect for traditional knowledge, ensuring that both the environment and cultural heritage are preserved.

Media and storytelling also play a crucial role in promoting environmental awareness through cryptid myths. Outreach programs that incorporate cryptid themes have the power to educate global audiences about the challenges facing our planet. These programs capture the public's imagination by positioning cryptids as ambassadors for biodiversity, making complex environmental issues more accessible and engaging. International campaigns harness the intrigue of cryptids to draw attention to conservation efforts, using storytelling to bridge cultural and geographic divides. These narratives resonate with audiences worldwide, inspiring action and fostering a deeper connection to the natural world.

The stories of cryptids, woven into the fabric of our cultures, offer a unique way to view conservation. They remind us of the wonders that lie beyond our understanding, urging us to protect the mysteries that enrich our world. Through these legends, we find inspiration to safeguard the ecosystems that sustain both the mythical and the mundane, preserving the delicate balance of life on Earth.

Rainforest biodiversity

9.2 CRYPTIDS AND BIODIVERSITY AWARENESS

Cryptid myths, with their allure of the unknown, are powerful symbols of biodiversity. Legends like Bigfoot and the Loch Ness Monster captivate our imagination, drawing attention to the wonders of unexplored ecosystems. They remind us of the rich complexity of life that exists beyond our immediate perception, urging us to look deeper into nature's hidden corners. These tales encourage curiosity and foster a sense of stewardship for the natural world. By spotlighting these mythical creatures, conservation campaigns can ignite interest in preserving lesser-known species and the interconnected ecosystems they inhabit.

Cryptids, in essence, become ambassadors for biodiversity, highlighting the importance of protecting the intricate web of life that sustains us all.

The influence of cryptid lore extends to scientific exploration, where it has prompted researchers to embark on expeditions in search of evidence.

While some quests may not uncover the mythical creatures themselves, they often lead to the discovery of new species, expanding our understanding of biological and ecological dynamics. These journeys into remote and uncharted areas reveal the vast diversity of life that thrives in hidden corners of our planet. Cryptozoology, though sometimes dismissed as pseudoscientific, has played a role in expanding the boundaries of biological exploration. By investigating reports of cryptid sightings, researchers contribute to the mapping of ecosystems and the identification of species yet to be classified. This field encourages a sense of wonder and curiosity, driving scientific inquiry into the mysteries that lie beyond the reach of conventional science.

Blending mythology and science in biodiversity protection presents both challenges and opportunities. Scientific studies often attempt to separate myth from reality, aiming to ground conservation efforts in empirical evidence. However, the role of folklore in complicating conservation priorities cannot be ignored. Cryptid legends, deeply rooted in cultural narratives, enrich our understanding of ecosystems while also presenting obstacles to scientific validation. These stories offer insights into the historical relationships between humans and the natural world. They remind us that conservation is not solely a scientific endeavor but also a cultural one, requiring us to consider the values and beliefs that shape how we interact with the environment. By embracing the complexity of these narratives, we can develop conservation strategies that honor both the scientific pursuit of knowledge and the cultural significance of the unknown.

As we navigate the intersection of fact and folklore, we find ourselves at a crossroads of understanding. Cryptid myths, with their blend of mystery and reality, invite us to explore the uncharted territories of our world with an open mind and a sense of wonder. They challenge us to look beyond the surface, to question our assumptions, and to embrace the complexities of the natural world. Through these stories, we discover the richness of biodiversity and the importance of protecting the ecosystems that sustain us. These mythical beings, or possibly real creatures, in their elusive and enigmatic ways, remind us of the enduring power of curiosity and the unyielding desire to uncover the secrets of the natural world. As we move forward, let us carry these lessons into the realms of the unknown that await in the following chapters.

TEN
EYEWITNESS ACCOUNTS AND MODERN SIGHTINGS

Nessie crossing the road next to Loch Ness as seen by George Spicer and his wife in 1933.

ON A SUMMER'S day in 1933, George Spicer, a respected businessman, and his wife drove along the northern shore of Scotland's Loch Ness. As their car rounded a bend, they caught sight of an extraordinary creature crossing the road ahead. Described as a large, undulating form with a long neck, the sighting astonished them. It began a worldwide fascination with what would become known as the Loch Ness Monster. This sighting, coupled with its vivid detail and credible witnesses, propelled Nessie into the global spotlight, sparking scientific investigations and a flood of curious visitors eager to glimpse the legendary beast for themselves.

1958 Bluff Creek Sasquatch tracks

10.1 EVIDENCE AND ENCOUNTERS--TO BELIEVE OR NOT BELIEVE?

In 1958, deep in the forests of Bluff Creek, California, a bulldozer operator named Jerry Crew found massive footprints in the dirt surrounding his bulldozer. Measuring 16 inches in length and 7 inches wide, these enormous prints were unlike anything seen before. They soon led to the name "Bigfoot." The prints were accompanied by other mysterious occurrences: a missing 50-gallon oil drum and a 700-pound spare tire thrown into a gully. Crew's discovery, accompanied by plaster casts of the footprints, captured the media's attention and sparked public intrigue. The possibility of a giant, bipedal creature roaming through the woods inflamed imaginations worldwide, laying the groundwork for the enduring mystery of Bigfoot. Shortly after the tracks were found, a fellow logger and prankster, Ray Wallace, hoaxed the world by making fake Bigfoot tracks with 16-inch carved wooden feet, which his family announced in 2002 after Wallace passed away at 84. However, experts agree that many of the original tracks were authentic since the carved wooden feet could not make the degree of detail found in many of the tracks and their casts.

· · ·

The evidence from these encounters continues to ignite debate. The Patterson-Gimlin film, captured in 1967, remains one of the most compelling pieces of evidence for Bigfoot's existence. Filmed by Roger Patterson and Bob Gimlin toward the end of an extended horseback trip in the same Bluff Creek area, it shows a large, apparently female (due to the presence of mammaries), hairy creature walking upright, eventually crossing a creek. Its movements have been extensively studied by experts, its steps measured, and measurements taken of the site to evaluate the creature's height compared to the trees. Skeptics have tried to debunk it, yet it remains a cornerstone of documentation for Bigfoot. Similar debates surround photographs and physical artifacts, such as plaster casts of footprints and hair samples. These items, while intriguing, often face scrutiny over their authenticity and the methods used to collect them.

Public perception is crucial in shaping the narrative of these cryptid sightings. Media portrayals, ranging from earnest documentaries to sensational headlines, influence how these stories are received and interpreted. Public fascination often clashes with scientific skepticism, creating a dynamic interplay that sustains the mystery. The media can elevate a cryptid to legendary status or cast doubt on its existence, depending on how a story is framed. This dual role of the media contributes to a culture where cryptids are celebrated and questioned, reflecting the human desire to believe in the extraordinary while seeking evidence to support those beliefs.

The lasting impact of these encounters on cryptid lore is undeniable. Iconic sightings like the Loch Ness Monster and Bigfoot have become touchstones in popular culture, inspiring countless books, films, and television shows. They fuel a cycle of curiosity and investigation, drawing new generations into the world of cryptids. These stories, passed down and retold, continue to inspire researchers and enthusiasts to seek out the unknown, keeping the spirit of exploration alive.

Reflection Section: Consider the Evidence

Take a moment to reflect on the iconic cryptid encounters discussed. Consider the evidence presented, such as the Patterson-Gimlin film or the casts of Bigfoot footprints. What do you find most compelling or questionable about these pieces of evidence? Why do you think these stories have endured in popular culture? Reflect on how your perceptions align with or differ from those of the general public.

Television was instrumental in disseminating early cryptid stories.

10.2 THE ROLE OF MEDIA IN CRYPTID SIGHTINGS

The influence of media on cryptid sightings cannot be overstated, as it plays a pivotal role in shaping both the narrative and public perception of these creatures. Historically, television and radio have been instrumental in disseminating cryptid stories, bringing them into living rooms and igniting imaginations. Programs dedicated to the unexplained, such as "In Search Of..." in the 1970s, captivated audiences with tales of creatures lurking on the fringes of reality. Often dramatized with eerie music and suspenseful narration, these shows left viewers curious and skeptical, eager for more. Newspapers and magazines have long chronicled cryptid sightings, providing a platform for eyewitnesses to share their stories and for journalists to explore the unexplained. From local papers reporting on mysterious tracks in remote woods to glossy magazines featuring in-depth analyses of alleged encounters, print media has been a constant vehicle for cryptid lore, blending fact with sensationalism to captivate readers and sell subscriptions.

• • •

As we transitioned into the digital age, the way cryptid sightings are reported and consumed underwent a dramatic shift. Online platforms and social media have revolutionized the sharing of cryptid encounters, allowing stories to spread farther and faster than ever before. Enthusiasts now flock to forums and groups dedicated to the unexplained, where they can exchange theories, share experiences, and debate the existence of these elusive beings. Platforms like YouTube and TikTok host countless videos purporting to show cryptids, offering people a vast array for viewing. Documentaries and reality TV shows have further fueled cryptid popularity. However, these portrayals are often sensationalized, crafted for entertainment rather than accuracy. The thrill of the hunt and the suspense of the unknown are woven into the narrative, blurring the line between fact and fiction. This entertainment-driven approach can skew perceptions, leading audiences to confuse dramatized content with genuine investigation. Often, when cryptid researchers are interviewed after filming, they admit they were compelled to act in a certain way for the camera's advantage rather than actually doing cryptid research in their preferred manner.

Misinformation and sensationalism present significant challenges in the media's coverage of cryptids. The proliferation of hoaxes and fabricated evidence is a persistent issue as individuals seek notoriety or profit from the public's fascination with the unknown. Fake photographs and doctored videos circulate widely, often going viral before their authenticity is questioned. Clickbait headlines and sensational stories further muddy the waters, enticing viewers with promises of definitive proof while delivering little more than speculation. The ease with which false information can spread online compounds these challenges, as viral posts reach global audiences almost instantaneously. Social media outlets are beginning to implement restrictions requiring labeling when using AI in social media. This should address some of the hoaxing issues and help viewers avoid confusion. However, this environment, rich with exaggerated claims, complicates the pursuit of credible information, leaving both the curious and the skeptical at a loss. This sensational allure often makes finding the truth more difficult.

Despite these challenges, the media plays an undeniable role in shaping cultural perceptions of cryptids. Through its lens, cryptids are portrayed as either credible phenomena worthy of investigation or mere folklore, relics of a bygone era. This dichotomy influences public attitudes, swaying them toward belief or skepticism. Media representation directly impacts the cultural mythology surrounding cryptids, as stories told and retold become part of the collective consciousness. Television shows, documentaries, and magazine articles contribute to the lore. Social media allows eyewitnesses to connect, fostering communities of people who can share their stories and sometimes heal from the trauma of terrifying experiences. This connectivity creates a rich collection of narratives that reflect the diverse ways people engage with the unknown. Through these presentations, cryptids remain alive in the public imagination, their stories evolving with each retelling, perpetuated by the media that narrates and presents them.

Eyewitness encounters can be terrifying and difficult to accurately recount.

10.3 ANALYZING EYEWITNESS TESTIMONIES

In cryptid research, eyewitness testimonies hold a unique place, offering both insight and challenge. With its complexities, the human mind plays a pivotal role in shaping these accounts. Psychological factors can profoundly influence how an experience is remembered and recounted. Fear, for example, can warp perception, casting shadows over the clarity of a memory. When someone catches a fleeting glimpse of a creature that defies explanation, their mind races to fill in the blanks, often embellishing details. This response is natural, driven by the brain's need to make sense of the unknown. Yet, it introduces complexity to these testimonies, requiring researchers to sift through embellished pieces, or what may be extraneous information, to uncover the truth.

Memory and perception are not static but dynamic processes that can shift over time. How a person recalls a cryptid encounter may evolve, influenced by subsequent discussions, media portrayals, or self-doubt. Memories can fade, merge, or become distorted, particularly when fear or excitement is involved. Because memories can be fluid, relying on them for evidence through eyewitness testimony can be challenging. However, these accounts are invaluable because although they may not be completely accurate due to many factors (dim lighting, fear, inaccurate memory), they usually contain aspects of truth that can guide further investigation. The key lies for the listener to distinguish between fact and fiction, which demands a combination of empathy and skepticism.

Evaluating the credibility of eyewitness testimonies involves careful analysis and a methodical approach. One technique is to identify consistent patterns across multiple accounts. When different witnesses describe similar features, behaviors, or circumstances, it adds a layer of credibility to their encounter stories. Cross-referencing testimonies can also reveal common threads that suggest authenticity. Interviews and empathetically asking relevant questions are essential, allowing researchers to evaluate a witness's experience more fully. By asking detailed questions and examining the consistency of their responses, investigators can assess the reliability of an account. This process should be done rigorously and respectfully, acknowledging that even imperfect memories can contribute valuable information.

Cultural and environmental factors further complicate the interpretation of cryptid sightings. Cultural beliefs and folklore heavily influence how witnesses perceive and describe their encounters. In regions where stories of mythical creatures are deeply embedded in the local culture, eyewitnesses may frame their experiences in ways that align with these narratives. Environmental conditions also play a significant role. Poor visibility in the dim light of dusk or during a heavy downpour can obscure details and lead to misidentification, which illustrates the importance of context in evaluating testimonies. Understanding the cultural backdrop and environmental conditions can provide crucial context that helps researchers interpret these accounts as accurately as possible.

Despite their challenges, eyewitness testimonies are indispensable in cryptid investigations. They often serve as the initial spark that ignites field research, guiding researchers to specific locations or phenomena. Eyewitness accounts can inform the direction of an investigation, suggesting where to look and what to seek. Integrating these reports into cryptid databases enriches the pool of information available to researchers, allowing for broader analysis and pattern recognition. However, much work remains to be done in this area. Building comprehensive databases that cross-reference and catalog testimonies could enhance our understanding of cryptids, offering new avenues for exploration.

Creating a safe space for individuals to share their eyewitness encounters is crucial. Many people hesitate to recount their experiences, fearing ridicule or disbelief. Platforms like podcasts offer an outlet for these stories, providing a judgment-free space where witnesses can speak openly. Often, this is the first time they feel heard and their experiences are validated. This nonjudgmental listening respects the individual's experience and enriches the collective understanding of cryptids. Encouraging open dialogue and fostering a supportive environment can uncover stories that might otherwise remain untold, adding depth and dimension to the study of these elusive creatures.

If you have a story to tell and haven't told it yet for fear of judgment or ridicule, reach out to a podcaster or a YouTube channel that is relevant to your story. There is someone else who can relate to you and share your story. You will feel much better when you have someone to talk to. *Of course, always ensure that the person or channel is safe and can be trusted.

Cryptid hunting with technical equipment.

10.4 CRYPTID HUNTING: MODERN EXPEDITIONS AND FINDINGS

In the dense forests of the Pacific Northwest in North America, where trees can grow up to 300 feet tall, and the undergrowth is thick, modern cryptid hunters embark on expeditions that push the boundaries of exploration. These expeditions focus on uncovering evidence of cryptids, particularly Bigfoot. Equipped with state-of-the-art technology, teams venture into the heart of these habitats, hoping to capture irrefutable proof of the creature's existence. Recent high-profile expeditions have drawn attention to regions known for frequent sightings, employing traditional tracking methods and cutting-edge innovations, such as thermal imaging and night vision goggles, which are particularly useful for nighttime tracking. This intersection of the old and new reflects a broader trend in cryptid research, blending the skills of seasoned trackers with the latest technological advancements.

On the other side of the Atlantic, the mystery of the Loch Ness Monster continues to draw investigators to its depths. Unlike the sprawling forests of North America, Loch Ness offers its own challenges—a vast expanse of deep, murky water hiding its secrets beneath the surface. Sonar devices send out waves that bounce off objects in the water, creating detailed images of what lies below, and have been used to search the Loch Ness. Side scan sonar utilized in 1975 provided a photo suggestive of a creature with a plesiosaur-like flipper. In 1987 and 2016, newer generations of sonar were used in major surveys. New variations of CHIRP sonar allow one to see 600 feet deep and to either side, allowing thorough exploration and detailing of deep water and the bottom of the loch. Alongside sonar, webcams around the loch provide real-time surveillance, capturing footage day and night. This continuous monitoring increases the likelihood of observing something unusual, contributing to the growing archive of potential evidence and allowing regular citizens monitoring the webcams to have a stake in "Nessie's" story.

In the field of cryptid hunting, technology plays a pivotal role. Drones have become essential tools for capturing aerial footage without navigating rugged terrain. They can cover large areas quickly, providing a bird's-eye view of potential habitats. Trail cameras, often motion-activated, are strategically placed to capture images of wild creatures without human interference. These cameras, equipped with night vision, operate silently, waiting for movement to trigger their shutters. DNA analysis and environmental sampling represent another frontier in cryptid research. Researchers can analyze genetic material for traces of unknown species by collecting samples from potential habitats, such as ponds, lakes, or the mud near caves. Thermal imaging cameras and sound recorders add another layer of sophistication, detecting heat signatures and capturing audio that might indicate a cryptid's presence. With all these tools available, researchers can potentially gather significant amounts of varied data to create a substantial body of evidence.

Despite technological advancements, cryptid expeditions face significant challenges. The locations where these creatures are believed to dwell are often remote and difficult to access. Dense vegetation can obscure trails, making navigation treacherous. In mountainous regions, altitude poses additional risks, with thin air and steep inclines testing the endurance of even the most experienced explorers. Weather conditions can shift rapidly, turning a promising expedition into a dangerous, even fatal, struggle against the elements. Sudden storms, heavy rains, and extreme temperatures complicate the logistics, requiring careful planning and adaptability. Yet, these challenges are part of what makes cryptid hunting so compelling. For many, it's the perfect combination of adventure, mystery, and excitement. For cryptid researchers, the possibility of discovery outweighs the risks, driving them to continue searching the wilderness.

Despite the obstacles, recent expeditions have yielded intriguing findings. In North America, teams have collected hair samples and recorded vocalizations that defy easy classification. These samples undergo rigorous analysis, with researchers examining their structure and composition to understand them better. In Loch Ness, sonar scans have revealed large, moving objects, sparking debate about what they could be. While definitive proof remains elusive, each piece of evidence adds to the body of knowledge, inspiring further inquiry.

Looking ahead, the future of cryptid hunting holds exciting possibilities. Emerging technologies like artificial intelligence could revolutionize data analysis, allowing for more accurate identification of patterns and anomalies. Interdisciplinary collaboration involves bringing together experts from various fields, such as biology, anthropology, and technology, and promises to enhance research efforts. By pooling knowledge and resources, these collaborations can tackle the complex questions surrounding cryptids, opening new avenues for investigation.

As we conclude this chapter, the exploration of hidden creatures continues to captivate and challenge. The blend of technology and human curiosity drives the search forward, inviting us to consider what might still lie undiscovered. In the next chapter, we delve into the cultural significance of cryptids, exploring how these legends reflect and shape our understanding of the world.

ELEVEN
CULTURAL SIGNIFICANCE AND COMPARATIVE MYTHOLOGY

Spooky legends are best shared at night.

IT'S at night when people want to share cryptid stories--especially gathered around a campfire, huddled around the kitchen table, in a back-yard tent by lamplight, or eating snacks together at a sleepover. That's when spooky, mysterious things seem to become real and take on more meaning than they might in the light of day. We whisper of creatures lurking in places just beyond the reach of light, where legends and reality blend. This chapter explores universal archetypes found in cryptid legends across cultures, revealing how these elusive beings reflect the shared fears, hopes, and mysteries of people around the world. Through the lens of folklore, we uncover the common threads that bind these tales together, offering a glimpse into the collective psyche that has shaped them.

The Kitsune

11.1 CRYPTID ARCHETYPES: SIMILARITIES ACROSS CULTURES

Certain archetypes emerge with remarkable consistency among the myriad cryptid tales around the world, transcending cultural boundaries and resonating deeply with human experience. One archetype is the Trickster, embodying chaos, cunning, and the unexpected. In Native American lore, the Pukwudgie is a prime example. These are small, usually 2-3 feet tall, mischievous creatures that look like little, hairy people. They came from the legends of the Lenape (Delaware) people in the Indiana area long before it was a State. They are known for playing tricks on humans but can also be dangerous, pushing people off cliffs, attacking them with knives and spears, and blinding them with sand in their eyes. Similarly, in Japan, the Kitsune, or fox spirit, is renowned for its shapeshifting abilities and playful deceit. The Kitsune, which can assume either male or female form, is extremely intelligent and can live up to 1,000 years. Both the Pukwudgie and Kitsune reflect a fundamental human fascination with the unpredictable elements of life, serving as reminders of the thin line between order and chaos.

· · ·

Another prevalent archetype is that of the Guardian. This protector watches over sacred spaces and significant natural features like rivers, hills, and plains. The Yeti, a legendary figure in Himalayan culture, is revered not merely as a powerful creature but as a guardian of the mountains, embodying the respect people hold for these awe-inspiring landscapes. Meanwhile, in Japan, the Kappa, a water-dwelling being, is a guardian of rivers and lakes, ensuring these systems stay balanced and protected. These guardian archetypes symbolize humanity's recognition of the need to protect and preserve the natural world.

These archetypes fulfill essential psychological and cultural needs, providing frameworks through which societies can make sense of the unknown. Cryptid myths offer explanations for phenomena that defy conventional understanding, serving as placeholders in the narrative of human discovery. By personifying the unexplained, these stories provide comfort. Furthermore, cryptid archetypes reinforce societal norms and taboos, using the fear of the unknown to instill caution and moral lessons. The Trickster teaches humility by challenging one's control. At the same time, the Guardian instills a deep respect for the sacredness and the beauty of the wilderness.

These archetypes have undergone significant transformation, adapting to the changes of cultures over time. Sea monsters, for example, have evolved from the terrifying creatures of ancient Greek mythology into the more familiar legends of today, such as the Loch Ness Monster. This evolution reflects a shift from viewing the sea as a frightening domain of chaos to a place where we can discover fascinating things. We can now even view the deep sea with excitement as there's so much yet to explore. Similarly, the werewolf legend, rooted in European folklore, has transformed from a tale of a cursed individual agonizing with dark magic into a personal "struggle of duality" story, resonating with contemporary themes of identity and self-acceptance.

With their rich array of archetypes, cryptids continue to captivate the human imagination. As you delve further into these legends, consider the universal themes they reveal about our shared humanity and the enduring mysteries that connect us all. Through this exploration, we find that the stories of cryptids are not just tales of hidden creatures but reflections of the human journey itself, offering insight into life's complex and ever-evolving landscape.

For an interesting article about the Kitsune, see Nana Young's 2024 article on Bokksu.com, Kitsune: The Enigmatic Fox of Japanese folklore.

For a few interesting and reasonably contemporary potential Pukwudgie sightings, see Peter Muise's blog http://newenglandfolklore.blogspot.com, A Pukwudgie Sighting in Massachusetts 4/22/23.

See Cheyenne Grimes' article on Pukwudgies if you'd like to read more and visit a popular location for sightings: Grimes, C. (2020, October 30). Pukwudgies and Where to Find Them. Indiana History. https://indianahistory.org/

The Werewolf in film, scaring a new generation of cinephiles.

11.2 THE ROLE OF CRYPTIDS IN MODERN CULTURE

Cryptids have a remarkable presence in modern culture, weaving into contemporary media and entertainment. Films and television shows demonstrate our fascination with these mysterious creatures, using them as a canvas to explore the unknown. Shows like "The X-Files" delve into the mysteries surrounding cryptids, blending science fiction with the allure of the unexplained. In "Harry and the Hendersons," Bigfoot symbolizes misunderstood nature, bringing to light themes of acceptance and coexistence. More recently, "Sasquatch Sunset" embraces the mystery and enchantment of cryptids, drawing audiences into a world where reality and legend intertwine. Video games also embrace cryptids, with titles like "The Witcher" series and "Disco Elysium," weaving them into intricate narratives that challenge players to question the boundaries between myth and reality. These digital realms allow players to engage with cryptid lore in interactive and immersive ways, making these creatures part of our collective cultural experience.

· · ·

Beyond entertainment, cryptids have infiltrated consumer culture, becoming icons that adorn a wide range of products and brands. Bigfoot, in particular, has emerged as a marketing icon, especially in outdoor and adventure brands. His rugged, mysterious image perfectly conveys the spirit of exploration and adventure, making him a staple in campaigns celebrating the great outdoors. Cryptid imagery appears on clothing lines and accessories, offering consumers a way to express their fascination with the unknown. From t-shirts adorned with playful renditions of the Loch Ness Monster to backpacks emblazoned with Sasquatch footprints, these products tap into the public's enduring curiosity and love for the mysterious. The commercial appeal of cryptids highlights how deeply they resonate with people, transcending their folkloric origins to become part of everyday life.

Cryptids also play a significant role in counterculture and subcultures, symbolizing rebellion, mystery, and the allure of the unknown. They are emblematic of the fringe, representing ideas and beliefs outside mainstream acceptance. This makes them popular symbols in alternative movements, embodying the spirit of questioning and challenging societal norms. Festivals and conventions dedicated to cryptids have sprung up, becoming vibrant hubs for enthusiasts to gather, share stories, and celebrate these enigmatic creatures. These events offer small business opportunities, as vendors sell everything from handcrafted cryptid art to themed merchandise. More importantly, they foster a sense of community, bringing together people from diverse backgrounds united by a shared interest in the world's mysteries. For many, these gatherings are more than just entertainment; they are a chance to connect with like-minded individuals and share stories and experiences. For many cryptid enthusiasts who only connect online, they are an opportunity to finally meet each other face-to-face. Regarding learning opportunities, some festivals offer expert speakers, scientific lectures, and opportunities to gather data.

In an educational context, cryptids are powerful tools for engagement and learning. Schools have begun incorporating cryptid myths into their curricula, using them to teach critical thinking and the importance of questioning evidence. By examining stories of creatures like Bigfoot or the Chupacabra, students learn to sift through folklore and fact, developing skills essential for navigating a world filled with information and misinformation. Cryptids also provide a gateway to exploring cultural diversity and global myths, offering insights into how different societies understand and interact with the unknown. Through cryptid narratives, students encounter the rich array of human storytelling, gaining an appreciation for the myriad ways in which cultures have sought to explain the unexplainable. This approach enriches their understanding of the world and encourages a sense of wonder and curiosity vital for lifelong learning.

Cryptids continue to captivate the imagination, transcending their origins to become integral to the cultural landscape. They challenge us to question, explore, and embrace the unknown. Whether through media, merchandise, counterculture, or education, cryptids remain vital to our shared human story, inviting us to ponder the possibilities beyond our understanding.

The Tanuki

11.3 COMPARATIVE ANALYSIS: CRYPTIDS AND GLOBAL MYTHS

Delving into the diverse world of global myths has shown that cryptids are central to many cultural stories and traditions. Consider the water monsters, like Scotland's Nessie and Australia's Bunyip. Both creatures dwell in the depths of lakes or billabongs, yet they emerge from distinct cultural contexts. Nessie, often depicted as a long-necked, serpentine figure, is steeped in Scottish lore, symbolizing the mystery of the deep and the unknown lurking beneath tranquil waters. On the other hand, the Bunyip holds a place in Aboriginal Australian stories, portrayed with varied forms but consistently embodying a guardian spirit of sacred waterways. Although both cryptids embody the mysterious nature of aquatic environments, they also act as cultural guardians, warning against disrespecting nature's boundaries.

Shapeshifting creatures, such as the Native American Skinwalker and the Japanese Tanuki, offer another fascinating comparison. The Skinwalker, rooted in Navajo tradition, is a spirit or creature capable of transforming into animals or humans at will, often associated with dark magic and malevolent intent. This figure embodies the fear of the unknown and the disruption of the natural order. People who report encountering the Skinwalker almost universally experience a feeling of dread or terror. Across the Pacific, the Tanuki of legend is a mischievous, transformative creature of Japanese folklore, known for its playful tricks and shapeshifting abilities. Unlike the sinister Skinwalker, the Tanuki is often portrayed with humor, reflecting a cultural embrace of the trickster spirit. The Tanuki is a Japanese raccoon dog, a real animal that lives in wooded land and is moving into urban areas, much like the raccoon in the United States. These shapeshifters highlight the cultural differences in how the transformation of a creature is perceived—either as a threat or a source of amusement.

Trade and exploration have significantly influenced cryptid narratives, spreading myths across continents and allowing them to evolve. The Silk Road, a historic trade network, facilitated the exchange of goods and ideas, including the pervasive dragon myth. Originating in China as symbols of power and prosperity, dragons found their way into European folklore, taking on more fearsome traits, often signifying chaos and danger. Similarly, European explorers brought their legends to the Americas, mingling with indigenous stories and creating new hybrid myths. The European werewolf, a creature of transformation and terror, influenced the tales of the Wendigo in North American lore. However, the latter has its roots in Algonquian mythology, where it embodies the dangers of cannibalism and insatiable greed. This cross-cultural exchange illustrates how myths adapt, absorbing elements from diverse traditions while retaining their core essence.

Adapting global myths into local stories is a testament to the fluidity and resilience of folklore. Once foreign to Western audiences, Eastern dragon myths have integrated into Western culture, transforming into the winged, fire-breathing dragons of medieval Europe. These adaptations reflect the exchange of ideas and the universal appeal of specific mythological themes, such as the fight between good and evil or the quest for power. The European werewolf myths have influenced the Wendigo, showing how stories change when cultures interact. This mix combines elements from both traditions, creating meaningful, rich stories across different times and places.

· · ·

Cryptids often mirror the values and concerns of their originating cultures. In societies with strong environmental values, guardian cryptids like the Yeti or Bunyip reinforce the importance of preserving natural habitats and respecting the delicate balance of ecosystems. These creatures serve as reminders of humanity's responsibility to protect the environment. Conversely, trickster cryptids thrive in cultures with rich oral storytelling traditions, reflecting societal fears and the unpredictability of life. Cryptids challenge social norms and show the dangers of pride or moral wrongdoing. These stories reflect the cultural values and concerns of the societies that created them, providing insights into shared human experiences.

The Thunderbird

11.4 CRYPTIDS AS CULTURAL NARRATIVES: STORYTELLING TRADITIONS

Cryptids have long been an intricate part of traditional storytelling, serving as conduits for conveying moral lessons and cultural wisdom. In Native American storytelling, cryptid tales often embody profound teachings, passed down through generations around the flickering glow of a campfire. These stories, rich in symbolism and meaning, serve as both entertainment and instruction, highlighting the values and norms of the community. For instance, tales of the Thunderbird, a powerful spirit bird, emphasize the importance of respect for nature and the consequences of disrupting the natural order. These narratives act as a moral compass, guiding listeners toward a deeper understanding of their place within the world and their responsibilities to it.

Similarly, in African cultures, cryptids play a pivotal role in the oral traditions upheld by griots, the revered storytellers and historians. With their vast repertoire of tales, the griots employ cryptid figures to teach social values and ethical lessons. Through stories of mythical creatures like the Mokele-Mbembe or the Nandi Bear, griots underscore themes of bravery, caution, and the balance between humanity and the natural world. These creatures, though elusive, become symbols of the unknown forces that shape human existence, inviting reflection and introspection. The oral tradition allows cryptid stories to adapt over time, keeping the stories relevant and meaningful with each telling.

As societies transitioned from oral to written traditions, cryptid stories found new life in literature, leaving an indelible mark on the literary landscape. Classic works such as "Beowulf" and "Journey to the West" feature cryptid-like beings, weaving them into epic sagas that explore themes of heroism, identity, and the struggle against the monstrous. In "Beowulf," the titular hero confronts Grendel, a creature of the shadows, embodying the archetypal battle between light and darkness. This tale, rooted in ancient myth, reflects the human confrontation with fear and the unknown. Similarly, "Journey to the West" introduces a host of fantastical beings, drawing on the rich tapestry of Chinese folklore to craft a narrative of spiritual and physical adventure. Through their depiction of cryptid figures, these stories have influenced modern fantasy and horror genres, inspiring countless adaptations and reinterpretations.

Cryptid myths also serve as vital vessels for preserving cultural heritage and safeguarding the stories and traditions that define a people. By maintaining indigenous languages and customs, cryptid tales contribute to the cultural revival movements that seek to reclaim and celebrate marginalized identities. In communities where traditional ways of life are threatened, cryptid narratives become a source of pride and resistance, affirming the unique perspectives and histories that have shaped them. Through these stories, cultures assert their enduring presence, ensuring that the wisdom of the past continues to teach and inspire future generations.

In contemporary storytelling and media, cryptids offer a lens through which to examine important issues and societal concerns. Environmental conservation, for instance, finds expression through cryptid narratives highlighting ecosystems' fragility and the need for stewardship. Stories of the Loch Ness Monster or the Yeti underscore the interconnectedness of human and natural worlds, advocating for the preservation of the unspoiled wilderness. Similarly, cryptids serve as metaphors for social and cultural conflicts, reflecting the tensions and aspirations of the societies that create them. In media, cryptid figures challenge audiences to confront their biases and assumptions, prompting dialogue and reflection on the complexities of identity and community.

Cryptids remain central to our stories about ourselves and our place in the world as we move forward. They embody the mysteries that elude us, the lessons we strive to learn, and the connections that bind us across time and space. In the next chapter, we will explore the future of cryptid research and its implications for science and society.

TWELVE
THE FUTURE OF CRYPTID RESEARCH

Drone with a pterodactyl-like cryptid

IMAGINE STANDING at the edge of a dense forest, ready to launch a drone high above the canopy after months of preparation. You've determined the appropriate habitat and season and calculated for good weather. You've borrowed, rented, or purchased expensive equipment to use and hopefully return without damage. This is not only fun; it's the cutting edge of cryptid research. Drones, equipped with high-resolution cameras and sometimes thermal imaging, allow researchers to explore vast and remote areas previously inaccessible. These aerial machines provide a bird's-eye view, capturing images and videos that might reveal the elusive creatures we search for. Their ability to cover large swathes of wilderness efficiently makes them invaluable in searching for aquatic, land-based, and even flying cryptids.

In the shadowy depths of dense jungles, thermal imaging cameras reveal secrets hidden from the naked eye. These devices detect heat signatures, allowing researchers to spot warm-blooded animals in areas of low visibility. This technology is beneficial in places like the Pacific Northwest, where sightings of creatures like Bigfoot often occur. Researchers can differentiate between known wildlife and potential cryptid evidence by pinpointing heat sources, making nighttime investigations more productive and less intrusive. The precision of thermal imaging offers a new level of insight, turning darkness into an ally rather than an obstacle.

Collecting water samples for eDNA

12.1 CRYPTID RESEARCH: TOOLS OF THE TRADE

In the depths of dense jungles or the dark of night, thermal imaging cameras reveal secrets hidden from the naked eye. They detect heat signatures, allowing researchers to spot warm-blooded animals in areas of low visibility. This technology is beneficial in places like the Pacific Northwest, where sightings of creatures like Bigfoot often occur. Researchers can differentiate between known wildlife and potential cryptids by pinpointing heat sources, making nighttime investigations more productive and less intrusive. The precision of thermal imaging offers a new level of insight; investigators can get an idea of a creature's size, shape, and location based on its heat signature. Thermal imaging has become the norm for researchers foraying into the darkness. It can be head-mounted for ease of use.

Genetic technology has revolutionized cryptid research, offering tools like environmental DNA (eDNA). eDNA can show what species are present, what the biodiversity of an area is, and if any invasive, endangered species or cryptids are present. As detailed by NOAA Ocean Exploration, this method involves collecting samples from environments where cryptids are rumored to exist and analyzing them for genetic material shed by creatures passing through. The promise of eDNA lies in its non-invasive nature, allowing scientists to gather evidence without direct contact.

DNA analysis, in general, is becoming more important and more common. Currently, it remains a costly form of scientific investigation, but as products become more available, costs tend to decrease. Portable DNA analysis equipment further enhances field research, enabling the quick processing of samples to avoid contamination. Collecting and processing DNA in the field is vital to obtaining meaningful results. Citizen scientists can be taught good techniques and contribute to the general body of knowledge of their cryptids of interest. Once adequate DNA data is obtained, correctly interpreting mitochondrial and nuclear DNA is crucial, as each provides unique insights into the organism's identity and lineage.

Virtual and augmented reality are set to transform public engagement with cryptozoology. Imagine putting on a virtual reality headset and stepping into a realm where you can experience cryptid encounters firsthand. These immersive experiences can educate and entertain, offering a taste of the thrill that drives cryptid hunters. Augmented reality apps take this a step further, allowing users to explore cryptid habitats in real time, overlaying digital information on their physical surroundings. This fusion of technology and cryptozoology invites a wider audience to participate in the search, fostering a deeper connection to the natural world.

Artificial intelligence, or AI, is another tool that reshapes the field. AI collects vast amounts of data from global wildlife networks, analyzing patterns and anomalies that might indicate cryptid activity. Machine learning algorithms process eyewitness reports and sightings, identifying commonalities that could point to genuine phenomena. These technologies will provide a level of analysis previously unattainable. As researchers use these to collect data and make them available in online communities, cryptid sighting areas will become more readily known around the world. We must use this information responsibly and not destroy the habitats of cryptids by rushing to sighting locations once they are known by many. AI will begin to offer new perspectives on old mysteries. As it continues to evolve, its role in cryptid research will expand, potentially helping illuminate the mysteries that have captured human curiosity for generations.

Reflection Section: Consider Your Role in Cryptozoology

Reflect on how you might contribute to the future of cryptid research. Whether through supporting scientific efforts, sharing stories, or fostering discussions, your actions can positively impact how people around you see the science of cryptids. Consider where your interests align with the technologies and approaches discussed and how you might engage with the ongoing quest to uncover the truth behind cryptids.

Slenderman

12.2 CRYPTIDS IN THE CURRENT AGE: INTERNET MYTHS

In the digital age, the internet has become a powerful engine propelling cryptid narratives into the public consciousness. Social media platforms and online forums teem with tales of mysterious creatures, each post contributing to an ever-growing narrative of modern folklore. Websites like Reddit host vibrant discussions where enthusiasts dissect sightings, share theories, and speculate on the existence of creatures like the Mothman or the Jersey Devil. These platforms amplify voices that might otherwise remain unheard, allowing cryptid stories to reach a global audience almost instantly. This democratization of storytelling, while exciting, also introduces new challenges, particularly the proliferation of misinformation and digital hoaxes.

In this dynamic landscape, the line between fact and fiction often blurs. Viral hoaxes, crafted with the intent to deceive or for pure entertainment, can spread rapidly, complicating genuine research efforts. The infamous case of Slender Man, an internet-born entity instantly adopted into popular culture, exemplifies this phenomenon. Initially created as part of a Photoshop contest, Slender Man quickly morphed into a cultural icon, sparking debates about the power of digital storytelling. These fabrications can overshadow legitimate cryptid research, casting doubt on authentic findings. Fact-checking websites have emerged as valuable tools to debunk false claims, restore credibility to the field, and provide clarity in a sea of information. Yet, the task remains daunting, as the vastness of the internet makes it impossible to control the narrative completely.

The evolution of digital storytelling has transformed not only what cryptid stories are told but how they are consumed. Podcasts and YouTube channels dedicated to cryptid lore offer in-depth explorations, blending interviews, expert insights, and dramatic reenactments to captivate audiences. Visual mediums, such as digital art and animation, bring these legends to life with vivid imagery, inviting viewers to experience cryptid encounters more fully. This multimedia approach engages audiences on multiple levels, appealing to both the analytical and the imaginative. It creates an immersive experience, drawing listeners and viewers into a realm where reality feels fluid.

Online communities play a crucial role in the collaborative nature of modern cryptid research. Enthusiasts worldwide converge in digital spaces to exchange information, analyze evidence, and support one another's investigations. Databases and archives dedicated to cryptid documentation grow through crowdsourcing, harnessing countless individuals' collective knowledge and experiences. Platforms like YouTube and podcasts provide forums for sharing sightings and theories. At the same time, crowdfunding sites like GoFundMe enable ambitious research projects to secure the financial backing needed. These digital avenues encourage cooperation, positivity, and inclusivity, ensuring that the quest for cryptids remains a vibrant and evolving endeavor.

You can be a part of the solution by avoiding participating in hoaxes. Hoaxes muddy the waters of actual investigatory findings and are difficult to disprove. They take energy away from investigations that work toward finding authentic evidence. They demoralize people in the cryptid community. If you want to be involved, join a platform and contribute positively.

. . .

There may be adventures in your area where you can go on cryptid explorations. In Forks, WA, you can join a Sasquatch habitat campout. In other places, you can hike and watch for their stick structures. Check out YouTube for excellent videos of Sasquatch stick structures; Colorado Bigfoot is a good example of a Sasquatch YouTube channel that can help you learn to recognize stick structures.

Academic clubs offer students opportunities to investigate cryptid myths.

12.3 THE NEXT GENERATION OF CRYPTID ENTHUSIASTS

The youthful fascination with cryptozoology is a testament to the enduring allure of the unknown, driven by the vibrant influence of pop culture. Movies and TV shows bring creatures like Bigfoot and the Loch Ness Monster to life. At the same time, video games and documentaries offer interactive and educational experiences that captivate young minds. Various media forms ignite curiosity, often leading individuals to explore deeper topics. Academic clubs and programs recognize this initial spark and offer structured environments where students can investigate cryptid myths. These settings enable students to engage with cryptid stories while improving their research skills and critical thinking abilities. Through these initiatives, young enthusiasts are encouraged to question, explore, and challenge the limits of accepted scientific knowledge.

Digital connections have further galvanized the next generation of cryptid enthusiasts, creating a web of shared interests and collaborative exploration. Social media groups, hashtags, and online forums have become bustling hubs where young minds gather to share ideas, theories, and artwork. Creativity and curiosity flourish in these spaces, allowing for the exchange of knowledge and perspectives that transcend geographical boundaries. Influencers and content creators have tapped into this vibrant community, transforming cryptid research into accessible entertainment. Bloggers, YouTubers, and podcasters produce content that resonates with younger audiences, inspiring them to get involved and stay informed. By weaving engaging and informative narratives, these creators play an important role in shaping the interests and understanding of their followers.

Cryptozoology clubs and online communities collectively nurture a generation eager to explore the mysteries of cryptids, fueled by a blend of imagination and inquiry. These platforms provide information and foster a sense of belonging among enthusiasts. As students share their findings or theories, they become part of a more extensive dialogue that values both skepticism and belief. This exchange often leads to a lifelong passion for exploration, where the pursuit of cryptids becomes a gateway to broader scientific discovery. The combination of traditional media and digital platforms allows for a dynamic and multifaceted strategy for cryptozoology that bridges generations and inspires continuous learning. The result is a thriving community of young cryptid enthusiasts ready to carry the torch of exploration into the future.

Students having fun while practicing observation and field research

12.4 CRYPTIDS IN EDUCATION

Imagine a classroom buzzing with excitement as students gather around a table to examine a cast of an unidentified footprint. Teachers worldwide are finding innovative ways to engage students by using cryptids as entry points for scientific inquiry. These legends provide a captivating framework for students to learn the scientific method. Students hone their analytical skills by formulating hypotheses, evaluating evidence, and distinguishing fact from fiction. Interactive classroom activities, like making footprint casts or mapping sightings, allow students to develop observation and reasoning skills. Debating the plausibility of cryptid claims requires critically examining evidence and encouraging students to question and explore.

Cryptid studies offer a unique blend of disciplines, making them ideal for cross-disciplinary learning. Educators can integrate these elements into biology, geography, history, and literature lessons, fostering a rich scientific and cultural exploration landscape. Competitions and creative projects, such as art contests or model-making challenges, provide opportunities for creative storytelling and collaborative problem-solving. These activities enhance creativity and build confidence as students learn to express and defend their ideas. As they dive into these projects, students experience the thrill of discovery, sparking a lifelong curiosity.

Modern tools for exploration and research are also becoming integral to education. Technologies like drones, motion-sensor cameras, and GPS tracking bring cryptid investigations to life, teaching students about data collection and field research. Hands-on fieldwork simulations, such as outdoor excursions or schoolyard surveys, allow students to explore natural environments and practice observational skills. These experiences instill a sense of wonder and respect for the natural world, emphasizing the importance of scientific inquiry. By engaging with these tools, students gain practical skills and a deeper understanding of the environments around them.

Cryptids also serve as a bridge to discussions on conservation and ecology. Educators can use cryptid narratives to discuss endangered species, biodiversity, and habitat preservation by connecting mythology to real-world science. These discussions encourage environmental awareness and stewardship, inspiring students to advocate for local conservation efforts. Projects like the one undertaken by fifth graders in Hoquiam, WA, who passed a resolution to protect Bigfoot, demonstrate how young minds can impact real-world conservation. Such initiatives foster a sense of responsibility and empowerment, as students learn the importance of preserving ecosystems, and put civics lessons to work in the real world through the legislative system.

Finally, cryptids can inspire students to pursue careers in biology, anthropology, paleontology, and environmental science. They serve as gateways to science and exploration, showing how curiosity about the unknown can lead to significant discoveries. Opportunities for students to present their findings at science fairs or in local media boost confidence and encourage ongoing engagement with scientific inquiry. As students explore these paths, they contribute to a future where the natural world's mysteries continue to inspire and challenge.

. . .

1. For educators, here is a list of five art projects related to cryptids suitable for 15-year-olds in the classroom. These projects will encourage creativity, research skills, and artistic expression.

1. **Cryptid Research and Illustration**
   1. Objective: Students will research a chosen cryptid and create an original illustration based on their findings.
   2. Materials Needed: Drawing paper, pencils, colored pencils, markers, reference books, or internet access.
   3. Steps:
      1. Each student selects a cryptid (e.g., Bigfoot, Loch Ness Monster, Chupacabra).
      2. Research the cryptid's history, sightings, and characteristics.
      3. Create an illustration that represents the cryptid, incorporating details from their research.
      4. Present the illustration to the class, sharing interesting facts learned during the research.
2. **Cryptid Diorama**
   1. Objective: Construct a diorama depicting a scene involving a cryptid in its natural habitat.
   2. Materials Needed: Shoebox, construction paper, modeling clay, paint, natural materials (twigs, leaves), glue, scissors.
   3. Steps:
      1. Choose a cryptid and research its supposed habitat.
      2. Use the shoebox as a base to create a three-dimensional scene.
      3. Construct the cryptid using modeling clay and place it within the diorama.
      4. Add details using natural materials and paint to enhance the scene.
      5. Share the diorama with the class, explaining the choices made for the habitat.
3. **Cryptid Storybook Creation**
   1. Objective: Write and illustrate a short story featuring a cryptid.
   2. Materials Needed: Blank booklets or sheets of paper, pens, colored pencils, markers, and binding materials.
   3. Steps:
      1. Develop a storyline involving a cryptid as a main character.

2. Write the story, paying attention to narrative structure and character development.
3. Illustrate each page to enhance the storytelling.
4. Bind the pages to create a finished storybook.
5. Read the storybook to the class, highlighting the creative process.

4. **Cryptid Mask Making**
   1. Objective: Design and create a wearable mask inspired by a cryptid.
   2. Materials Needed: Cardboard, paper mâché, paint, elastic bands, scissors, glue.
   3. Steps:
      1. Research the physical features of a chosen cryptid.
      2. Sketch a mask design that incorporates these features.
      3. Use cardboard as a base and build up features with paper mâché.
      4. Paint the mask to bring the cryptid to life.
      5. The students can use the mask to illustrate a relative cryptid legend if they choose to.

5. **Cryptid Mural Collaboration**
   1. Objective: Collaboratively create a large mural depicting various cryptids.
   2. Materials Needed: Large canvas or paper, paint, brushes, markers.
   3. Steps:
      1. Divide the class into groups, with each group selecting a different cryptid.
      2. Plan the mural layout and decide on the placement of each cryptid.
      3. Each group paints their section of the mural, focusing on their chosen cryptid.
      4. Combine the sections to create a cohesive mural.
      5. Display the mural as a collaborative art piece in the classroom or school hallway.

These projects foster artistic skills and enhance students' research abilities, collaboration, and storytelling, making cryptids an exciting theme for classroom art activities.

· · ·

2. Here are five scientific projects suitable for 16-year-olds. These projects involve cryptid research and use creeks, woods, cameras, computers, the internet, and regular school supplies. They integrate various scientific disciplines and encourage critical thinking and analysis.

1. **Cryptid Mythology vs. Biology**
   1. Objective: Compare the mythological descriptions of a cryptid with known biological species, examining how real animals can influence folklore.
   2. Materials Needed: Reference books, internet access, comparison charts.
   3. Steps:
      1. Choose a cryptid and gather detailed mythological descriptions.
      2. Identify real species that share similar characteristics (e.g., giant squids for Kraken legends).
      3. Create a comparison chart highlighting similarities and differences.
      4. Discuss how certain animal behaviors or appearances could inspire cryptid myths.
      5. Present a paper or presentation on the findings.
2. **Biodiversity Survey and Cryptid Indicators**
   1. Objective: Conduct a biodiversity survey to explore how a rich ecosystem might support cryptid myths.
   2. Materials Needed: Cameras, identification guides, notebooks, internet for research.
   3. Steps:
      1. Choose a site in the woods or by the creek to survey.
      2. Document and identify various species of plants, insects, birds, and mammals.
      3. Research any local cryptid myths and compare their features with documented species.
      4. Hypothesize how misidentification or rare sightings of certain species might contribute to cryptid legends.
      5. Create a report or presentation with species lists and potential cryptid connections.
3. **Wildlife Monitoring with Trail Cameras**
   1. Objective: Use trail cameras to monitor wildlife activity and analyze how it might relate to cryptid sightings.

2. Materials Needed: Trail cameras, computers for reviewing footage, and notebooks.
3. Steps:
    1. Set up trail cameras in strategic locations within the woods or near the creek.
    2. Record wildlife activity over a period of weeks.
    3. Analyze footage for unusual or rare animal behavior.
    4. Discuss how such behaviors could be interpreted as cryptid sightings.
    5. Compile findings in a video presentation, highlighting interesting footage and analyses.
4. **Acoustic Monitoring for Cryptid Calls**
    1. Objective: Record and analyze natural sounds to investigate claims of cryptid vocalizations.
    2. Materials Needed: Audio recorders, computers with sound analysis software, and notebooks.
    3. Steps:
        1. Set up audio recorders in the woods to capture natural sounds over several nights.
        2. Use sound analysis software to identify and categorize animal calls and other natural sounds.
        3. Research cryptid myths involving vocalizations (e.g., Bigfoot howls, tree knocks, whistles) and compare them with recorded sounds.
        4. Discuss possibilities of misinterpretation or unknown species contributing to cryptid vocalization reports.
        5. Present findings using audio samples and analysis charts, highlighting key discoveries.
5. **Cryptid Sightings Data Analysis**
    1. Objective: Analyze cryptid sighting reports to identify patterns or anomalies.
    2. Materials Needed: Access to cryptid databases, spreadsheets, and graphing tools.
    3. Steps:
        1. Collect data on reported sightings of a specific cryptid over a set period.
        2. Input data into a spreadsheet and categorize by location, time, and description.
        3. Use graphing tools to identify patterns, such as clustering in certain areas or times of year.

4. Hypothesize potential explanations for these patterns, considering factors like environmental changes or human activity.
5. Share the analysis through a presentation, highlighting key insights.

These projects incorporate fieldwork, data collection, and analytical skills, allowing students to use different sciences, including ecology and biology, to explore and learn about folklore and cryptid myths hands-on.

3. Here is a list of 5 civics projects for 14-year-old students, focusing on cryptids while integrating civic education concepts. Each project aims to enhance students' understanding of civic responsibility, ways to engage with the community, and the intersection of culture and belief.

1. Cryptids and Indigenous Perspectives

1. Objective: Explore how Indigenous cultures view cryptids and their significance in cultural narratives.
2. Materials Needed: Folklore texts, interviews with Indigenous community members, research articles, and presentation software.
3. Steps:
4. Research specific cryptids that are part of Indigenous folklore (e.g., the Wendigo or the Thunderbird).
5. Identify and develop respectful interview questions to ask Indigenous community members about their perspectives on these legends.
6. Create a comparative analysis of Indigenous narratives and Western interpretations of the same cryptids.
7. Develop a presentation highlighting the importance of respecting Indigenous knowledge and perspectives in understanding cryptids.
8. Facilitate a discussion on the role of cultural narratives in shaping community values.

2. Cryptid Legislation and Ethics Discussion

1. Objective: Explore the ethical implications and potential legislation surrounding the protection of cryptid habitats.

2. Materials Needed: Research materials on environmental law, articles on cryptids and conservation, and debate guidelines.
3. Steps:
4. Research existing laws that protect wildlife and habitats.
5. Choose a specific cryptid and study its purported habitat and ecosystem.
6. Discuss the implications of protecting such habitats, considering scientific perspectives and community beliefs.
7. Organize a classroom debate on the ethics of protecting mythical creatures versus verified endangered species.
8. Write a reflection on what you learned about the balance between folklore, ecology, and law.

3. Cryptids in Media and Public Perception

1. Objective: Analyze how media representation of cryptids influences public perception and belief in these creatures.
2. Materials Needed: Access to various media (books, films, documentaries), analysis templates, and presentation tools.
3. Steps:
4. Select a few media representations of a specific cryptid (e.g., Bigfoot in movies).
5. Examine how these portrayals differ from traditional descriptions and impact public beliefs.
6. Discuss the role of media in shaping cultural narratives and how misinformation can spread.
7. Create a visual presentation or infographic summarizing findings and your thoughts on the media's influence on belief in cryptids.
8. Host a class discussion on the responsibility of media creators when depicting folklore and myths.

4. Cultural Significance of Cryptids Across the World

1. Objective: Investigate the cultural significance of cryptids in various societies and their roles in folklore and tradition.
2. Materials Needed: Research materials, presentation software, and cultural study templates.
3. Steps:
4. Choose a selection of cryptids from different cultures (e.g., Yeti from Nepal, Mokele-Mbembe from Congo).

5. Research each cryptid's role in its culture, including historical significance and modern interpretations.
6. Create a comparative chart that highlights similarities and differences in beliefs and stories.
7. Prepare a presentation to share findings with the class, discussing what these legends reveal about the cultures they come from.
8. Reflect on how understanding diverse perspectives on cryptids can foster respect and appreciation for different cultures.

5. Cryptids and Environmental Policy

1. Objective: Explore how cryptid legends can influence conservation efforts and environmental policy in local areas.
2. Materials Needed: Research articles, case studies, policy analysis tools, and internet access.
3. Steps:
4. Identify a local cryptid and research its associated habitat and environmental concerns.
5. Investigate current environmental policies affecting the region and how they relate to habitat preservation that might support that cryptid.
6. Create a presentation that discusses the importance of local biodiversity and how the cryptid could serve as a symbol for conservation efforts.
7. Propose a community initiative that promotes both cryptid awareness and environmental conservation.
8. Present the initiative to the class or local community group.

These projects encourage students to engage with their communities, explore cultural narratives, and think critically about the intersection of folklore, cryptozoology, and civic responsibility.

A bioluminescent squid in the abyss

12.5 THE FUTURE: CRYPTIDS AND THE UNKNOWN

Our world still has boundaries of discovery that stretch endlessly, where the secrets of our planet whisper through unknown forests and the depths of unexplored seas. Advances in genetics, imaging, and environmental monitoring pave the way for discoveries that may finally provide evidence of creatures once relegated to the realm of myth. New technologies allow us to glimpse previously hidden ecosystems, revealing life forms that challenge our understanding of biodiversity and evolution.

As we explore further, we will probably find that some cryptids are not mere figments of imagination. Tools like AI modeling and deep-sea explorations could reveal hidden habitats, changing our perception of remote ecosystems.

Cryptid myths evolve along with societies. As new cultural narratives take root, these legends adapt and change, reflecting contemporary situations, concerns, and aspirations. In an age dominated by digital media and speculative fiction, cryptid stories find new life in creators' imaginations who blend tradition with innovation. These tales are reimagined through movies, virtual reality, and interactive storytelling, capturing the essence of the legends while engaging audiences in new ways. This integration into popular culture ensures that cryptid stories stay relevant, serving as mirrors of our collective hopes and fears. Cryptid stories will continue to evolve and take on new meanings in the future. New internet-based cryptids may be created as our society shifts and new ideas and concerns develop. As society grapples with environmental degradation and technological advancement, cryptids symbolize the unknown forces we can't predict or control.

The pursuit of cryptids has always been a delicate balance between curiosity, belief, and skepticism. While the mystery of these creatures fuels our interest, scientific inquiry demands evidence and critical analysis. The challenge lies in maintaining this balance, preserving the allure of the unknown while upholding rigorous investigatory standards. Encouraging a mindset that values both imaginative exploration and empirical evaluation is crucial. Cryptid research can inspire creativity and foster a spirit of discovery, urging us to question our assumptions and embrace the possibilities of the unexplored. Navigating this terrain requires a commitment to credibility as well as creativity, ensuring the fascination with cryptids continues thriving.

The allure of the unknown has always pulled us, drawing people from all walks of life to pursue discovery. Cryptid myths, with their captivating stories and mysteries, continue to inspire art, storytelling, and scientific exploration. They ignite the imaginations of students, artists, and scientists, challenging them to dream and explore. The mysteries these legends embody serve as catalysts for creativity, propelling us to seek answers and unravel the enigmas that surround us. As we look to the future, the enduring appeal of cryptids promises to motivate the next wave of researchers and adventurers, urging them to venture into the unknown.

Protect nature's wonders

. . .

Cryptids of the World, Where Legends Meet Reality

Now that you have explored the fascinating world of cryptids, it's time to share your discoveries and help other readers embark on their own journey.

Simply by leaving your honest opinion of this book on Amazon, you'll guide fellow cryptid enthusiasts to the information they're looking for and help them pursue their passion.

Thank you for your help. The folklore and stories of cryptids live on when we pass on our knowledge – and you're playing an important role by providing a review.

Thanks so much!

REFERENCES

1. Greek Myths & Modern Cryptids https://paleothea.com/mythical-creatures/greek-myths-modern-cryptids/
2. The (Mostly) Unseen World of Cryptids: Legendary Monsters ... https://www.mdpi.com/2076-0787/13/1/1#:~:text=The%20close%20kinship%20of%20folklore,untrod%20paths%20in%20monster%20studies
3. The Beginnings of Cryptozoology – SciU - IU Blogs https://blogs.iu.edu/sciu/2021/01/23/the-beginnings-of-cryptozoology/
4. Schrope, M. (2013, January 14). Giant Squid Filmed in its Natural Environment. Nature. https://doi.org/10.1038/nature.2013.12202
5. History of Cryptozoology Timeline - Cryptid Wiki - Fandom https://cryptidz.fandom.com/wiki/History_of_Cryptozoology_Timeline
6. ZooChat. (2021, September 15). Examples of Island Gigantism. Retrieved from https://www.zoochat.com
7. The Beginnings of Cryptozoology – SciU - IU Blogs https://blogs.iu.edu/sciu/2021/01/23/the-beginnings-of-cryptozoology/#:~:text=He%20is%20considered%20the%20scholarly,the%20founding%20figures%20in%20cryptozoology
8. Beyond Bigfoot: the Science of Cryptozoology https://news.mongabay.com/2012/03/beyond-bigfoot-the-science-of-cryptozoology/
9. Gerber, W. (n.d.). Wes Gerber. Sasquatch Chronicles.
10. https://itunes.apple.com/WebObjects/MZStore.woa/wa/viewBook?id=0 This material may be protected by copyright.
11. Barackman, C. [Cliff], & Fay, J. [James Bobo Fay]. (n.d.). Cliff Barackman. Bigfoot and Beyond.
12. https://itunes.apple.com/WebObjects/MZStore.woa/wa/viewBook?id=0 This material may be protected by copyright.
13. Exploring Cryptid Habitats and Ecosystems https://hangar1publishing.com/blogs/cryptids/cryptid-habitats-and-ecosystems?srsltid=AfmBOoqbtCewgQ3L0Xzs_IbatEatPOc_7WGVxr1Skfr2KI-9BeqzPGIG
14. Genetics of Sasquatch: Making Cryptozoology Scientific? https://neuwritesd.org/2022/01/27/genetics-of-sasquatch-making-cryptozoology-scientific%EF%BF%BC/
15. Meldrum, J. (2007). Sasquatch: Legend Meets Science. Forge Books.
16. BFRO Geographical Database of Bigfoot Sightings \u0026 Reports https://www.bfro.net/gdb/
17. Mothman of Point Pleasant, West Virginia | Folklife Magazine https://folklife.si.edu/magazine/mothman-point-pleasant-west-virginia
18. Michigan Dogman https://en.wikipedia.org/wiki/Michigan_Dogman
19. Spooky Sight. (n.d.). 10 Shocking Mothman Sightings from 1966 to 2024. Retrieved February 1, 2025, from https://www.spookysight.com/10-shocking-mothman-sightings-1966-2024
20. The Jersey Devil and Folklore - Pinelands Preservation Alliance https://pinelandsalliance.org/learn-about-the-pinelands/pinelands-history-and-culture/the-jersey-devil-and-folklore/#:~:text=The%20most%20widely%20held%20belief,it%20was%20a%20baby%20devil
21. Williams, A. (2010). Enoch: A Bigfoot Story. CreateSpace.
22. Loch Ness monster | History, Sightings, \u0026 Facts https://www.britannica.com/topic/Loch-Ness-monster-legendary-creature

23. The Beast of Bodmin - Myth or Reality? https://www.bodminjail.org/blog/historical-tales/beast-of-bodmin/#:~:text=In%201995%20the%20Government%20ordered,no%20evidence%20against%20it%2C%20either

24. Before America Had Witch Trials, Europe Had Werewolf Trials https://www.history.com/news/werewolf-trials-europe-witches

25. Leprechaun | Lucky Charm, Pot of Gold & Irish Mythology https://www.britannica.com/art/leprechaun

26. Uncovering the Great Himalayan Mystery: the Yeti https://www.tibettravel.org/tibetan-people/himalayan-mystery-yeti.html

27. Ward, T. (2022, February 18). That Time Edmund Hillary Set Out in Pursuit of the Yeti. Mother Jones. Retrieved from https://www.motherjones.com

28. YouTube Archive. (n.d.). 1960 Yeti Hunting with Sir Edmund Hillary [Video]. YouTube. Retrieved February 2, 2025, from https://youtu.be/WMxauu_VAug?si=XllMf9gZQDp-MPKx

29. Ningen (folklore) https://en.wikipedia.org/wiki/Ningen_(folklore)

30. Mongolian Death Worm https://en.wikipedia.org/wiki/Mongolian_death_worm

31. Lebronmovie233. (2024, March 13). The Legend of the Mongolian Death Worm Unveiled [Video]. TikTok. Retrieved February 2, 2025, from https://www.tiktok.com/t/ZT26X7cDw/

32. Kappa (folklore) https://en.wikipedia.org/wiki/Kappa_(folklore)

33. Mokele-Mbembe: The Truth Behind Africa's Mythical River ... https://science.howstuffworks.com/science-vs-myth/strange-creatures/mokele-mbembe.htm#:~:text=However%2C%20Mokele%2DMbembe%20sightings%20continue,long%20neck%20and%20massive%20size

34. Marozi - Wikipedia https://en.wikipedia.org/wiki/Marozi#:~:text=Though%20there%20were%20local%20East,in%20the%20mountains%20of%20Kenya

35. Jinn: Who are the supernatural beings of Arabian and ... https://www.middleeasteye.net/discover/jinn-islamic-arabian-tradition-supernatural-beings

36. Grootslang https://en.wikipedia.org/wiki/Grootslang

37. Bunyip | Aboriginal, Dreamtime, Australia https://www.britannica.com/topic/bunyip

38. The Maero: Bigfoot in New Zealand Folklore https://www.ancient-origins.net/unexplained-phenomena/maero-bigfoot-new-zealand-folklore-009633

39. The Legend of Night Marchers in Hawai'i https://www.hawaiimagazine.com/the-legend-of-night-marchers-in-hawaii/

40. No'eau Woo-O'Brien. (n.d.). Hauka'i Po (Night Marchers) [Video]. YouTube. https://www.youtube.com/watch?v=89

41. Yara-ma-yha-who - Wikipedia https://en.wikipedia.org/wiki/Yara-ma-yha-who#:~:text=The%20Yara%2Dma%2Dyha%2Dwho%20is%20said%20to%20live,and%20then%20takes%20a%20nap

42. Chupacabra - Wikipedia https://en.wikipedia.org/wiki/Chupacabra#:~:text=The%20first%20reported%20attack%20eventually,reportedly%20completely%20drained%20of%20blood

43. El Silbón https://en.wikipedia.org/wiki/El_Silb%C3%B3n

44. Mapinguari https://en.wikipedia.org/wiki/Mapinguari

45. La Llorona: Reclaiming the Cautionary Tale https://www.latimes.com/delos/story/2023-10-16/la-llorona-mexico-latin-america-horror-folklore

46. Could Bigfoot and Sasquatch Outlive Humans? Survival ... https://www.southernstylesweettees.com/blog/jan-2

47. How the Search for Mythical Monsters Can Help ... https://therevelator.org/mythical-monsters-conservation/

48. The Power of Stories: Conservation through Traditional ... https://ioraecological.com/

the-power-of-stories-conservation-through-traditional-storytelling-in-meghalayas-indige
nous-communities/

49.   The Ecological Importance of Folklore https://voicesforbiodiversity.org/articles/the-
ecological-importance-of-folklore-shaping-our

50.   10 Weird Historical North American Monster Sightings https://listverse.com/2019/01/
31/10-weird-historical-north-american-monster-sightings/

51.   Media Messages and Public Beliefs about Cryptozoology https://ijoc.org/index.php/
ijoc/article/download/21417/4444

52.   O'Connor, J. (2024, February 6). The hoax that led to the word Bigfoot. Mental Floss.
https://www.mentalfloss.com/article/hoax-bigfoot

53.   Cryptozoology: The Search for Hidden Creatures https://www.academicblock.com/
science/fringe-science/cryptozoology#:~:text=Eyewitness%20Reliability%3A%20Eyewit
ness%20testimony%2C%20a,the%20credibility%20of%20reported%20encounters

54.   'Cryptid Tourism': worth the trip? https://aiptcomics.com/2023/12/01/cryptid-tourism-
bigfoot-mothman-ufo-uap/

55.   How Cryptids Influence Scientific Exploration https://hangar1publishing.com/blogs/
cryptids/cryptids-influence-on-scientific-exploration#:~:text=The%20Cultural%20Signifi
cance%20of%20Cryptids,humans%20and%20the%20natural%20world

56.   Courthouse Libraries BC. (2024, May 9). Sasquatch in BC law. Courthouse Library.
https://www.courthouselibrary.ca

57.   Exploring Cryptids and Human Evolution: Unraveling the ... https://hangar1publishing.
com/blogs/cryptids/cryptids-and-human-evolution?srsltid=
AfmBOopVJO5nsOoVHGVmo2J3pxvzdN8yK_pyte2GUvQXKlS4MB3kUCfz

58.   Modern Mythologies: The Culture of Cryptids - Sword & Shield https://uhsswordand
shield.com/26823/opinion/modern-mythologies-the-culture-of-cryptids/

59.   Mystical Creatures in Global Folklore Compared: A Cross- ... https://www.connollycove.
com/mystical-creatures-in-global-folklore/

60.   Exploring Cryptid Detection Technologies: Tools for ... https://hangar1publishing.com/
blogs/cryptids/cryptid-detection-technologies?srsltid=AfmBOoqr2wvif3hANomx0-
P9MzIs94Xtd2ihQYVw_7WoRYugdYxHV99z

61.   Environmental DNA (eDNA) - NOAA Ocean Exploration https://oceanexplorer.noaa.
gov/technology/edna/edna.html

62.   Media Messages and Public Beliefs about Cryptozoology https://ijoc.org/index.php/
ijoc/article/download/21417/4444

63.   Muise, P. (2023, April 22). A Pukwudgie Sighting in Massachusetts. New England Folklore. http://newenglandfolklore.blogspot.com

64.   Grimes, C. (2020, October 30). Pukwudgies and where to find them. Indiana History.
https://indianahistory.org/

65.   Creepy Cryptids And Where To Find Them https://www.trillmag.com/life/social-
media/creepy-cryptids-and-where-to-find-them/

66.   Colorado Bigfoot. (12 C.E., November 12). [Video]. Colorado Bigfoot.

67.   Graham, T. (n.d.). The Trickster Animal Spirit: Tanuki. Japan House. https://japanhouse-
.illinois.edu

68.   National Oceanic and Atmospheric Administration. (n.d.). Environmental DNA (eDNA).
NOAA Ocean Explorer. https://oceanexplorer.noaa.gov/home/science_technology/explo
ration_tools/edna.html

69.   National Oceanic and Atmospheric Administration. eDNA Fact Sheet. https://oceanex
plorer.noaa.gov/home/science_technology/exploration_tools/edna.html

ABOUT THE AUTHOR

Karen E. Mueller, DVM was born and raised in the Pacific Northwest. Besides being a cryptid student and believer, Dr. Mueller has two primary passions in veterinary medicine: improving the lives of pets through reducing and preventing pain and preventing the single most common cause of death in companion animals: euthanasia due to overpopulation. She has worked tirelessly in high-quality, high-volume, low-cost spay and neuter programs to address and prevent this problem. She continues to work in these programs through the region, as well as practice at Mueller Animal Chiropractic. She hopes to help pet parents help their pets, through her new website PetHealthHarbour.com.

You can connect with her or see what's new at:

https://pethealthharbour.com

 facebook.com/pethealthharbour
 tiktok.com/@Karen%20E.%20Mueller,%20DVM

www.ingramcontent.com/pod-product-compliance
Lightning Source LLC
Chambersburg PA
CBHW061754120626
46550CB00005B/2000